Bacon

Hobby Farms® Presents · Volume 11K · 2014

Editor in Chief
Amy K. Hooper

Senior Associate Editor
Annika Geiger

Associate Art Director
Kari Keegan

Cover Design
Veronique Bos

Production Coordinator
Leah Rosalez

Contributing Photographers
Kevin Fogle, Fiona Green, Amy Grisak,
Paulette Johnson, Kristen Lee-Charlson,
Patricia Lehnhardt, Sheila Nielsen

Editorial, Production and Corporate Office
3 Burroughs
Irvine, CA 92618-2804
949-855-8822
fax: 949-855-3045

Sales Offices
500 N. Brand Blvd., Ste. 600
Glendale, CA 91203
213-385-2222
fax: 213-385-0335

477 Butterfield, Ste. 200
Lombard, IL 60148
630-515-9493
fax: 630-515-9784

BACON is published by I-5 Publishing, 3 Burroughs, Irvine,
CA 92618-2804. Corporate headquarters is located at
3 Burroughs, Irvine, CA 92618-2804.

i-5 publishing
Imagination • Innovation
Insight • Inspiration • Integrity

MARK HARRIS, Chief Executive Officer; NICOLE FABIAN, Chief
Financial Officer; JEFF SCHARF, Chief Sales Officer; JUNE
KIKUCHI, Chief Content Officer; BETH FREEMAN REYNOLDS,
Vice President, Consumer Marketing; JENNIFER BLACK, Vice
President, Digital; MELISSA KAUFFMAN, Digital General Man-
ager; LISA MACDONALD, Marketing Director; LAURIE PANAG-
GIO, Multimedia Production Director; CHRISTOPHER REGGIO,
Book Division General Manager; CHARLES LEE, IT Director;
CHERRI BUCHANAN, Human Resources Director

Registration No.: R126851765
Part of the Hobby Farms® Presents Series
Printed in the USA

APR 2015

D1129270

Open Your MIND and Your Mouth

By Amy K. Hooper

the word "adventurous" struck a colleague as an odd choice when applied to bacon. He's the perfect candidate to look through this issue — because there is So Much More to cured and smoked pork than the typical breakfast serving or a BLT sandwich.

Count me among the aficionados who love to talk about "meat candy." One of my first destinations at the county fair is the vendor with the deep-fried chocolate-covered bacon. Oh, my goodness. My fondness for this food isn't limited to the dressed-up version, though. I will try just about anything decorated with bacon.

Have you seen comedian Jim Gaffigan's declarations about bacon as "the most beautiful thing on Earth"? When he calls bacon bits "the fairy dust of the food community" that improve everything and turn a salad intro an entree, I have to nod my head. Don't you?

We hope that you'll nod your head often — as in, "Yes! THAT is going to happen" — while perusing these recipes. We've got you covered from morn-ing to night, including desserts and cocktails.

You'll also find de-tailed instructions for making your very own bacon. You read that right: home-made bacon. Turns out just about any-one can create it. Turn to page 18 right now. What are you waiting for?

PATRICIA LEHNHARDT

Bacon

82

16

Cover image by Brent Hofacker/ Shutterstock

THE TASTY HISTORY of Bacon

More than a recent trend, this meat transcends time and continents.

BY SAMANTHA JOHNSON

once upon a time, bacon wasn't an integral part of international cuisine. During those barren days many centuries ago, the irresistible delight of bacon didn't exist as we know it today and that perfect pair "bacon 'n eggs" consisted of nothing but … eggs!

But from whence did the glorious idea of bacon originate? In what burst of brilliance did the concept of a cured pork product occur? Let's explore the history of our favorite meat product.

The Early Days of Bacon

According to the Online Etymology Dictionary, the word "bacon" dates to the 14th century and can be defined as "meat from the back and sides of a pig." It is said to be an Old French word derived from the Proto-Germanic "bakkon" meaning "back meat." The related word "flitch" refers to a "side of bacon" and is said to

date from 13th century Middle English, which indicates that the consumption of bacon in Europe predates the 13th century.

But long before the word "bacon" existed, the Chinese were curing and preserving pork as early as 1500 B.C., while another precursor to bacon — a dish called petaso — was regularly eaten in the Roman Empire. "Thousands of years ago, bacon came about as a food simply as a survival tactic," says Heather Lauer, author of "Bacon: A Love Story" (William Morrow). "People needed the ability to preserve meat and out of that was born the best meat ever."

Bacon drips with history and has been eaten by different cultures through many centuries.

According to Alan Davidson's "Oxford Companion to Food" (Oxford University Press), the word "bacon" was originally a generic term for any type of pork. By the 17th century, the word was reserved for its current (and more specific) definition.

As early interest in bacon grew, so did the focus on raising pigs with the characteristics to produce the best bacon. In Joseph Harris' 1883 book "Harris on the Pig" (reprinted by Lyons Press in 1999), he notes that the cross of the Berkshire pig with the Tamworth pig produces "the most profitable bacon pigs in the kingdom, [with] the Berkshire blood giving an extraordinary tendency to feed, and securing the early maturity in which alone the Tamworth breed is deficient." (Elsewhere in his book, Harris adds that "A well-cooked cheek of bacon, with roast chicken, is a dish for an epicure.")

Lauer notes that as other methods for preserving food became available in modern times, the relevance of bacon became driven more by flavor. "It just tastes good and it binds us together as a culture in a lot of ways," she says, "whether simply as a breakfast food or more unusually through the various ways in which it has become a 'trend' in recent years. It's unlikely that the people who originally figured out how to cure bacon could have imagined someone would one day dip it in chocolate!"

> TRUE OR FALSE: *It's recorded that people have been raising pigs in China as a food source since 7000 B.C.*
>
> ANSWER: *True. The oldest known recipe for pork, suckling pig stuffed with dates, comes from 500 B.C. China.*

Bringin' Home the Bacon

For centuries, the relative ease of pig-keeping meant that farmers had the opportunity to use bacon as an inexpensive way to feed their families, and in the United States during the 1800s and early 1900s, pork (including bacon) outranked beef as the most commonly eaten meat. Raising, processing and preserving one's own bacon was as economical as it was nourishing.

The first commercial bacon-processing facility was established by John Harris in 18th century England, and commercially produced bacon began to take off in the United States during the early 20th century. Advertisements from the era indicate a movement that encouraged housewives to cook with commercially produced bacon. "An easy economy — a side of Premium bacon," boasts one 1922 ad from Swift's Premium Hams and Bacon, while a 1930 ad references the "evenly proportioned" balance of "fat and lean" along with the "sanitary wrappings" in which the bacon was sold.

Despite its worldwide popularity and its long and impressive history, the appearance, flavor and style of modern-day bacon varies by geographic location. "The bacon that we know in the United States is actually quite different from the bacon you find in England and other parts of the world," Lauer says. "American bacon comes from the belly, but in other countries it's usually from the loin or sometimes also the shoulder. Loin bacon is much leaner, but it's still that tasty combination of sweet and salty flavors that happens in the curing process that makes it delicious. And I think it's complementary to a lot of different cuisines — there aren't many foods that can't be improved with bacon."

When you cure and smoke pork at home, you join a centuries-old tradition.

DEDEK/SHUTTERSTOCK

Once you've perfected the standard uses for bacon, try it in less traditional ways — such as covered in chocolate!

Bacon Today

Today, bacon is more popular than ever, as evidenced by the "bacon mania" that has taken hold of America over the past several years. According to a report on bacon trends released by National Pork Board in Des Moines, Iowa, "Over half of all households (53%) report that they always have bacon on hand in the kitchen (2005)," and "overall bacon consumption has remained stable over time. It is consumed an average of 18 times per person per year." Nowadays, consumers are most likely to enjoy bacon as part of a breakfast meal, and 75 percent consume bacon "as-is" rather than as an ingredient in a dish.

"I think you could argue bacon is at its peak popularity these days, although I would never call it a 'trend' — something that has been around for thousands of years isn't a trend," Lauer says. "The difference now is the Internet.

"Before the Internet, love of bacon was discussed in private and occasionally on television,"

she adds. "Now it's so easy for us to share our love of bacon with friends and strangers alike through blogs and social media… Due to the nature of social media, that has led to a contest of sorts to see who can do the craziest thing with bacon and get attention for it."

Lauer adds that the increased number of restaurants that offer "bacon-centric" promotional activities stem from marketing teams that saw the rising interest in all things bacon. "And as a result, bacon has become a 'trend' that won't die," she adds. "It's just too good for us to let that happen."

Samantha Johnson is the author of several books, including "The Beginner's Guide to Beekeeping" (Voyageur Press). She lives on a former dairy farm in northern Wisconsin with a Pembroke Welsh Corgi named Peaches, and she writes frequently about pets, gardening and food: http://samantha johnson.contently.com

diggin' into BACON

Diagram of a pig with labeled cuts:

- ear
- tusks
- shoulder
- boston butt
- ribs
- spareribs
- center loin
- tenderloin
- rump
- ham
- bacon
- shank end
- foot
- hock

How much do you know about the common styles of this pork product?

BY JENNIFER MACKENZIE

it's difficult just to call all cured pork belly "bacon." Many elements — from the cut to the processing, curing, flavoring and smoking (or lack thereof) — create different characteristics, making different styles. Let's explore some of the most common styles of pork bacon.

O-S-C-A-R: Bavarian immigrant Oscar Mayer first sold pre-sliced, packaged bacon in 1924.

Traditionally a slab of pork belly is cured with dry rub.

A dry rub or dry cure preserves the meat by removing moisture.

ER_09/SHUTTERSTOCK

Side bacon (also called regular, standard or American bacon; streaky bacon in Britain): Traditionally a slab of pork belly is cured with a dry rub, which generally consists of salt, nitrites (may or may not be used), sugar and/or honey or maple syrup, and spices for several days to draw moisture out of the meat, helping to preserve it. This also infuses the meat with flavor. The slab is then hung, or set out on racks to dry, followed by smoking at a moderately low temperature, which enhances the flavor, adds the characteristic smoky taste and has a preserving effect.

Commercially made bacon is commonly wet-cured by injecting brine into the pork belly, technically called "pumping." Less commonly, the belly might be immersed in brine. Both methods add water to the salt, nitrites and spices — which speeds up the curing process and bulks up the weight. The U.S. Department of Agriculture's Food Safety and Inspection Service sets limits for the amount of added liquid that can remain in the cured pork. Instead of heat smoking, the cured belly is sprayed with liquid smoke derived from smoldering wood chips. This product has a much higher water content, and the yield of cooked bacon is much lower than the dry-cured, naturally smoked product.

Side bacon is generally sold in slices, also called strips. Thin-cut bacon yields about 35 slices per pound, while regular-cut bacon yields 16 to 20 slices per pound. Typically side bacon is half to two-thirds fat by weight. High-quality side bacon has long strips of pink meat interspersed with fat streaks.

Slab bacon: Before it is sliced, slab bacon is sold as a slab, or a piece of the slab. This cut is handy for recipes that use diced pieces, lardons or large chunks.

Center-cut: Regular side bacon is cut from the whole belly, while center-cut bacon uses only the meatier, center section of the belly, resulting in a higher-quality bacon with a higher proportion of meat to fat.

Thick-cut: premium side bacon that yields 12 to 16 slices per pound

The Smoke

Different smoking techniques and woods used for smoking add distinct flavors to bacon. These are some of the most common treatments.

Double-smoked bacon is smoked as usual, then cooled and smoked again. This adds a deep smoky flavor and is particularly good for use in recipes where you want a rich smokiness. Home bacon makers and specialty smoke houses also do triple-smoked bacon.

Peameal bacon now is known as "sweet pickled pork loin" in Canada.

Commercially made bacon is commonly wet-cured by injecting brine into the pork belly.

Hickory gives a sharp, woody smoke flavor to bacon, while applewood and cherrywood give a mellow and sweet smokiness. Maple bacon might be cured with maple syrup and/or smoked over maple wood or processed with added maple wood flavor. Some commercially prepared brands use artificial maple flavor. Maple adds a sweet element to the salty, smoky bacon.

Other Varieties

Lower-sodium: Cured with less salt, and often less sugar, it typically has about 30 percent lower sodium content than regular bacon.

"Uncured" or "natural": Often labeled as "natural," uncured bacon is made without added nitrites but does have nitrite-containing naturally ingredients. This bacon must be labeled with "no nitrates or nitrites added except for those naturally occurring in ingredients such as celery juice powder, parsley, cherry powder, beet powder, spinach, sea salt, etc." The flavor does tend to be milder than conventionally cured bacon.

Other Cuts

Canadian bacon (also called back bacon): boneless pork loin trimmed of all visible fat, shaped into a round, then cured and smoked. More like ham than side bacon, this very lean type is a popular item on pizza and eggs Benedict.

Peameal bacon: This is boneless pork loin pickled in a salt brine and characterized by the bright pink meat surrounded by a thin layer of fat and vibrant yellow crust of cornmeal. The coating used to be made from peas, thus the name. In Canada, this product now must be labeled "sweet pickled pork loin" and is not called bacon. Peameal bacon is sold as chunks of the loin or in thin slices.

English bacon: boneless pork loin with a generous trim of fat that is cured and smoked. This is a fairly lean, meaty cut sold as chunks of the loin or in slices. The slices in Britain are called "rashers."

Pancetta: Italian bacon made from pork belly and cured similarly to side bacon but not smoked. The pork belly is rolled, jelly-roll style, into a cylinder before curing, then dried. The bacon lends a salty pork flavor without the typical smoke of other varieties. High-quality pancetta has equal parts meat and fat. It is generally sold in chunks of the cylinder or in thin slices.

A professional home economist, Jennifer MacKenzie (jennifer mackenzie.net) owns FoodWorx and creates cookbooks.

HOGS at the TROUGH

Choosing the source of your bacon is just as important as choosing the cut or flavoring.

BY LISA MUNNIKSMA

if it's true that you are what you eat, it only makes sense that the richest-tasting bacon comes from hogs that eat the most diverse feeds. It also makes sense that pigs developed for bacon production — for the quality of their belly muscle and fat — will provide superior bacon. In today's grocery-store-bacon society, however, some consumers have been led away from these principles.

Bacon Breeds

In general, commercial hog production favors pigs that have been selected for fast growth and lean meat. Lean meat isn't what gives bacon its flavor; neither does fat. The best bacon flavor and texture comes from a combination of lean muscle and well-developed fat.

There are lard-pig breeds and there are "baconers," explains Rob Levitt, co-owner of The Butcher & Larder whole-animal butcher shop in Chicago. Every bacon maker will have his or her own opinion about the best bacon breed. The Tamworth, for example, has a long body — and therefore a long belly, meaning a lot of

bacon-producing potential — and is often called "the bacon pig." At Levitt's shop, they prefer a Berkshire-Duroc cross: "We like them because they have a nice ratio of meat to fat."

Black Pig Meat Co. — owned by Duskie Estes and John Stewart, who also own Zazu Kitchen + Farm in Sebastopol, California — sources the majority of its bacon from Pure Country Pork, an Oregon farm that raises Chester White pigs in hoop-house systems. Depending on where on the belly the bacon is cut, Stewart gets an average of 30 percent fat in his bacon, which is ideal for him, because "I'm definitely looking to have the meat part of it expressed."

Common breeds raised for slaughter include Yorkshire, Duroc and Tamworth.

IVAN ANTONINO/SHUTTERSTOCK

Want to know more about butchering hogs? Turn to page 26.

NECK CHOPS LOIN CHOPS SHOULDER RIBS HAM JOWL BACON BACON

PAULETTE JOHNSON

Belly up! Most of the bacon strips seen in American stores today come from the belly of a hog, but bacon can come from the back and sides, too.

Stewart also raises Red Wattle and Mulefoot heritage-breed hogs and crosses, about 10 at a time, at his California home. He makes bacon on a small scale with these pigs. "I really like the fat on the Red Wattle," he says. "It's pretty close to beef fat."

Production Systems

Pigs raised in confinement — as commercially produced pigs are in the United States — don't have the opportunity to develop muscle fibers and flavors in the same way as pigs raised outdoors. These animals are surprisingly intelligent and social — two traits that lead to the development of negative behaviors, such as tail chewing and aggression, when pigs are kept in confinement.

"Getting them back outside as much as possible, even if it's in a hoop barn, is better for the pig, better for the environment and better all around," Stewart says.

When managed properly in a sustainable-farming system, pigs raised on pasture or in woodlots don't have the concentrated manure buildup found in industrial-hog facilities; require fewer antibiotics; are not stressed from close confinement; are able to indulge in their natural "pigginess" — roaming, rooting around in the soil, wallowing in mud and foraging for foods found in nature — and can contribute to a healthy woodland ecosystem and productive multispecies grazing system, which are boons for farmers and land managers. In addition to adding to overall farm health, this exercise and the foraged foods develop the meat and enrich the flavor of the pork.

"Winter pigs taste different than summer pigs," Levitt says. "It's the same thing with beef and lamb." One of the farmers who supplies The Butcher & Larder with pigs lets his animals graze in a fruit and chestnut orchard. "In November, you can really taste the fruitiness and the nuttiness," Levitt continues. These are flavors you won't find in commercial pork, which is most often fed a ration consisting of corn, soybean meal and minerals.

Pig to Table

Finding pasture-raised pork from different breeds isn't as easy as going to the grocery store. There are options, though, if you're willing to do some homework. As is the case with tomatoes (consider the taste and texture of an in-season tomato from your yard versus one shipped across the country out of season), meat tastes better when there are fewer steps between production and consumer.

"Try to start with whoever is local to you," Stewart says. "There are going to be people who make good things, and there are going to be people who make terrible things." Don't buy in bulk until you know you'll like it!

Try the local farmers market or co-op grocery store, and directly contact small-scale farmers.

"Find a source that is focused on where their animals are coming from," Levitt says. "There are a lot of decent bacon producers out there, but if they're just buying [confinement-raised pork] bellies, it doesn't mean anything to me."

If purchasing bacon sourced from local farmers isn't an option, look to your local butcher, and learn about the sources of his meats. With a growing interest around the world in understanding food sources plus an unwavering interest in bacon, there's always the Internet. Then you can taste-test bacon sources side by side to find the breed and the production system that suits your palate best.

Every bacon maker will have his own opinion about the best bacon breed.

Freelance writer Lisa Munniksma assists with caring for heritage-breed hogs on a farm in Kentucky. She is learning about sustainable living, agriculture and food systems around the world and writes about it at www.freelance farmerchick.com

Less confinement leads to healthier hogs, according to educators and the U.S. Department of Agriculture.

ROBERT BRUCE LILLEY/SHUTTERSTOCK

Tips for Cooking Perfect Strips

You have options beyond the frying pan.

By Cheryl Morrison

bacon can be fried, grilled, baked or nuked. Using any of those methods, you can produce straight strips that are evenly cooked just to the degree of crispness — or softness — that you prefer.

Baking and Grilling

Most restaurants cook bacon in the oven, which produces excellent results more efficiently than frying. Many home cooks also favor this method, which is easier and less messy than frying.

At the Bavarian Inn in Shepherdstown, West Virginia, bacon "goes into our convection oven for 7 to 9 minutes at 425 degrees," says sous chef Tim Durst. "That cooks it most of the way. Then we drain the fat off." The bacon is returned to the oven for a couple of minutes when orders come in, with the temperature depending on the order. "We can always bump it up for someone who wants it extra crispy," he says.

The cooks at Minerva's Restaurant & Bar in Rapid City, South Dakota, use a combination of baking and grilling. "We parcook it in the oven at 350," says executive chef Farzad Farrokhi, "about two-thirds of the way. We finish it on the grill. It takes three or four minutes to finish. Then we shake the fat off with tongs."

Farrokhi says he and his wife use their oven for cooking bacon at home, too. "It doesn't make a mess," he says, "and you don't get that residual bacon smell in the house that you get with frying."

Clair's Family Restaurant in Morgantown, Pennsylvania, uses wood-smoked slab bacon from a local producer and cooks it on a flat-top grill.

"We lay it out on the grill, flip it once and cook it three-quarters of the way through," says owner Clair Stanley. "Then we put it a cooling rack and let the grease drain." For each customer order, "we put it back on the grill to make it crisp" or just to heat it through for customers who prefer soft bacon. "If the customer wants it extra crispy, we'll put a weight on it, just for a few seconds."

Oven-cooked bacon creates less of a mess than other methods.

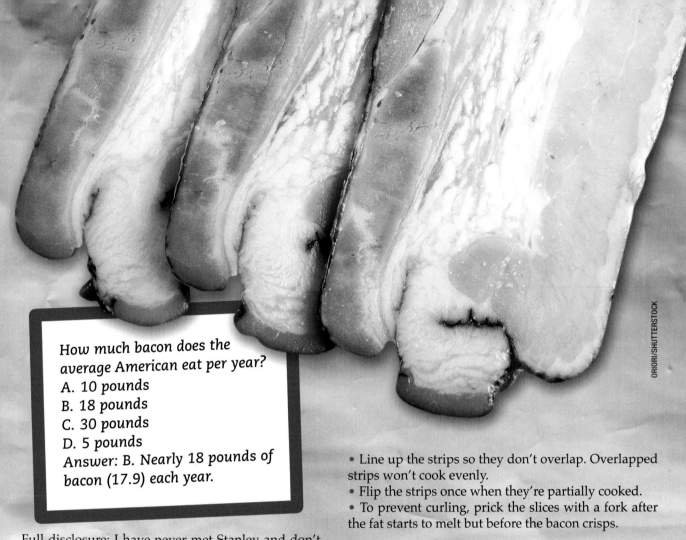

ORIORI/SHUTTERSTOCK

How much bacon does the average American eat per year?
A. 10 pounds
B. 18 pounds
C. 30 pounds
D. 5 pounds
Answer: B. Nearly 18 pounds of bacon (17.9) each year.

Full disclosure: I have never met Stanley and don't know anyone who has, but I've eaten breakfast at her restaurant a couple of times, and the bacon was perfect.

At home, I cook bacon in a gas oven, which I preheat to 350 degrees Fahrenheit while arranging the strips side by side on a shallow baking tray. Ten minutes into the cooking, I remove most of the grease from the tray, turn each strip with tongs, and turn the tray 180 degrees. When my nose tells me they're done, I move the strips to a plate lined with a couple of paper towels to degrease it. It's almost as delicious as Clair's, except that the raw bacon I use isn't quite as good.

Tips:
• For easier cleanup, line the baking tray with aluminum foil.
• To promote crispness, use a baster to remove grease from a baking tray during cooking.
• Arrange the bacon on a slotted broiler tray with a catch tray under it, eliminating the need to remove the grease.

Pan Frying

Many home cooks prefer to prepare their bacon in a pan on the stove, despite the splatters. Here are some tips for those who do:
• Start with a room-temperature pan. Cold bacon slapped into a hot pan is apt to burn.
• Cook a panful of bacon, not just a few strips, so you produce enough grease to prevent burning.

• Line up the strips so they don't overlap. Overlapped strips won't cook evenly.
• Flip the strips once when they're partially cooked.
• To prevent curling, prick the slices with a fork after the fat starts to melt but before the bacon crisps.

Microwaving

Cooks in a hurry can use microwave ovens to turn out crisp, tasty bacon with minimal mess. Lay paper towels on a plate, arrange the bacon strips on them side by side, and cover them with another paper towel before closing the door and pressing the start button.

One minute per slice on the oven's high setting is the rule of thumb, but watch it closely the first time; microwaves vary in power, and you might need to adjust the time. Also, if your microwave lacks a rotating tray, rotate the dish halfway through the cooking.

General Cooking Tips

Take the bacon from the refrigerator a half-hour before cooking it. This makes it easier to separate the slices.

Pay close attention when cooking bacon. Its thickness, the method used to cure and other factors — such as the evenness of your oven heat — can affect cooking times.

Strain and save the fat for use as cooking oil. It's loaded with flavor that shouldn't go to waste.

Slab bacon often comes with the rind still attached. The rind should be removed before you cook the bacon, but you can fry the rind separately to render it and produce cracklings, which make a delicious snack.

Cheryl Morrison, a freelance writer who lives in New York City and southern Vermont, cooks her bacon in the oven until it's crisp.

Bacon
MAKIN'

CURE

BUY

SMOKE

CUT

all bacon tastes delicious. No doubt about it. But have you ever bit into a crispy-on-the-outside, tender-on-the-inside, sweet-and-salty slice of smoky homemade bacon? If so, chances are good that you'll never go back to a store-bought variety.

What makes home-made taste so delectable? You can season the meat to your preferred saltiness. You can slice pieces to your desired thickness. You can add as much or as little smoke as you want. You can infuse the bacon with customized-for-your-palate flavors, like rosemary, black pepper, honey or maple syrup.

Plus, if you have a bacon-eating habit, making your own can save you a pretty penny.

With a fresh piece of pork belly, a few sweet-savory seasonings, a few tools and some know-how, it's easy to cure and smoke bacon at home. Even if you lack a traditional smoker, you can create some crackly goodness using liquid smoke and your oven. When there's a will, there's a way.

Here's everything you need to know to cure and smoke your own bacon at home.

Meat Market

Bacon as Americans know and love it is made from pork belly, a boneless cut of fatty meat from the belly of a pig. It features a layer of skin (though this might be removed), thick ribbons of silky fat and streaks of reddish-pink meat. Depending on the animal and the cut, a typical pork belly will weigh around 10 to 15 pounds.

Where do you find these fine chunks of meat? You likely will have a hard time finding one at your neighborhood grocery store, so you have several options. You can call a pork grower nearby who raises pasture-raised pigs and purchase an ultra-fresh belly; visit your local butcher or specialty meat market and ask the staff to order one for you; or check out an Asian grocery store, which will sometimes have it on hand.

Wherever you get the belly, make sure it has been properly handled, advises William Stringer

This cured pork has been rinsed and now rests on a rack before going into the refrigerator to form a pellicle.

Raw pork belly is cut into 2-lb. slabs, ready for dry rub or brine.

with the department of food science and nutrition for University of Missouri Extension.

"Begin with fresh bellies that have been chilled to below 40 degrees Fahrenheit within 24 to 30 hours after slaughter," he says. "If the bellies are purchased from a commercial source, they have been properly chilled. If the source is farm slaughter, take care to chill them rapidly."

Once you have your piece of pork belly and are ready to begin the curing process, prepare the meat by trimming it to your desired shape and weight. Use a wide, stiff-bladed knife, and cut the belly into uniform slabs; 2- or 4-pound hunks work well for DIYers, and the smaller cuts give the cure and smoke more surface area to penetrate.

Curing and Seasoning

The next bacon-making step is the curing process. Curing involves dry-rubbing or brining meat in a salt-sugar-nitrite-seasoning combination — aka the "cure" — for the purpose of preservation, flavor and color, says Brian A. Nummer, Ph.D., of National Center for Home Food Preservation at University of Georgia Extension.

"The cure ingredients can be rubbed on to the food surface or dissolved in water as in a brine," he says. "In the latter process, the food is submerged in the brine until [it is] completely covered."

Salt's starring role in the curing process is to draw moisture out of the cells of dangerous bacteria — like *Salmonella*, staphylococcus and *Listeria monocytogenes* — and to prevent their growth, Nummer says. This becomes especially important during the smoking process.

"Salt inhibits microbial growth by plasmolysis," he explains. "Water is drawn out of the microbial cell by osmosis due to the higher salt concentration outside the cell. The salt concentration needed depends on the genus and species of the microorganism. Fortunately, the growth of many undesirable organisms normally found in cured meat is inhibited at relatively low concentrations of salt."

Sugar then offsets some of the saltiness. "Because of the tremendous amount of salt used in curing bacon, sugar serves to reduce the harshness of the salt in cured meat and enhance the sweetness of the product," Nummer says.

Nitrites, found in commercially prepared cure mixes, are used to inhibit the growth of *Clostridium botulinum* spores — the microorganisms that

Know the Danger Zone

When handling your raw and cooked bacon, keep an eye on the temperature.

Microorganisms thrive in temperatures ranging from 40 to 140 degrees Fahrenheit. Pork kept in this temperature range for longer than two hours might become host to many species of foodborne illness-causing bacteria, including *Salmonella*, campylobacter, staphylococcus and *Clostridium botulinum*. Pork is also susceptible to harmful parasites, like *Toxoplasma gondii* and *Trichinella spiralis*.

Practice proper food-safety protocols when making bacon:

- While curing your bacon, keep it below 40 degrees F.
- While smoking/cooking your bacon, keep it above 140 degrees F.
- Make sure the internal temperature of your bacon reaches 160 degrees F when cooking.
- Do not leave the pork at room temperature for longer than two hours.

In addition, practice good hygiene by washing hands with soap and running water before handling food, and washing and sanitizing kitchen implements and countertops.

It's better to be safe than sorry! — R & W.W.

Cured pork is placed on hooks before going into the smoker.

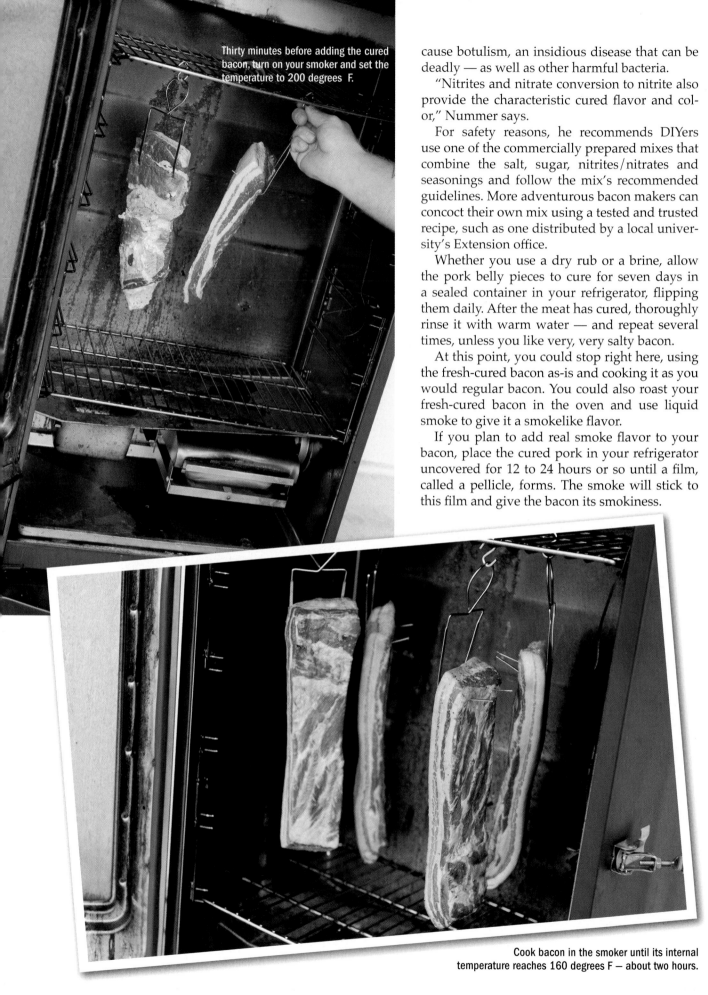

Thirty minutes before adding the cured bacon, turn on your smoker and set the temperature to 200 degrees F.

cause botulism, an insidious disease that can be deadly — as well as other harmful bacteria.

"Nitrites and nitrate conversion to nitrite also provide the characteristic cured flavor and color," Nummer says.

For safety reasons, he recommends DIYers use one of the commercially prepared mixes that combine the salt, sugar, nitrites/nitrates and seasonings and follow the mix's recommended guidelines. More adventurous bacon makers can concoct their own mix using a tested and trusted recipe, such as one distributed by a local university's Extension office.

Whether you use a dry rub or a brine, allow the pork belly pieces to cure for seven days in a sealed container in your refrigerator, flipping them daily. After the meat has cured, thoroughly rinse it with warm water — and repeat several times, unless you like very, very salty bacon.

At this point, you could stop right here, using the fresh-cured bacon as-is and cooking it as you would regular bacon. You could also roast your fresh-cured bacon in the oven and use liquid smoke to give it a smokelike flavor.

If you plan to add real smoke flavor to your bacon, place the cured pork in your refrigerator uncovered for 12 to 24 hours or so until a film, called a pellicle, forms. The smoke will stick to this film and give the bacon its smokiness.

Cook bacon in the smoker until its internal temperature reaches 160 degrees F — about two hours.

"Happily, bacon is very easy to make at home. ...Furthermore, what you make at home will be superior to just about anything you buy at supermarkets. Most of the bacon there comes from factory-raised hogs, the curing done at commercial plants, and the result is thin strips of watery meat that, even when cooked until crisp, have a taste only reminiscent of real bacon. When you make your own bacon and fry a slice, you'll know what bacon is all about." — Michael Ruhlman and Brian Polcyn, "Charcuterie" (W. W. Norton & Company)

Smoked bacon hangs in the refrigerator to be cooled before slicing.

Adding Smoke

In food preservation lingo, "smoking" meat can refer to preserving food (via smoke cooking or cold smoking) or flavoring food. For our DIY bacon-making purposes, we're doing the latter — adding smoke for flavor using a hot smoking process.

"Hot smoking is done in the smokehouse or more modern electric kilns, usually over a short period of time, just until the meat is cooked," Nummer says. "The meat is cooked and smoked at the same time over a burning fire or electric elements of a kiln."

Smokers for DIYers come in a range of styles and price points. According to Barbara Rasco, senior food scientist with Washington State University's Extension office, the main features a smoker should have are:

- an independent source of heat for the pot of wood chips or logs;
- a controllable vent or flue at the top;
- a controllable draft at the bottom;
- Thermostatic control over the oven temperature; and
- another heat source to raise the temperature in the smoker to 225 degrees F.

Before you pop your cured, pellicle-covered bacon into the smoker, prepare the meat by drying off any residual moisture, which can combine with the smoke to impart a bitter flavor.

About 30 minutes before you begin smoking the bacon, turn on the smoker, and set the oven's temperature to 200 degrees F. At the same time, get your wood smoking. Hickory is the standard wood type to use for smoking bacon, but just about any hardwood will do, including maple, oak, alder, birch and fruit woods like apple.

Once the oven reaches the right temperature, put your bacon in the smoker. You can hang the slabs on hooks or put them on racks, depending on your setup. Next, insert a meat thermometer into the fattest part, and cook the bacon until its internal temperature reaches 160 degrees F, which takes about two hours.

You can freeze your bacon for easier slicing.

A meat slicer helps you consistently cut bacon to your preferred thickness.

Cool, Slice and Enjoy

As soon as your bacon has reached 160 degrees Fahrenheit, pull it out of the smoker, place it on a platter, and let it chill out in your refrigerator until it's cool enough to handle. At this point, you have the option of slicing a slab and cooking some of your savory creation (highly recommended — you need to taste-test what you've done, right?) or saving it for later.

A meat slicer makes quick and easy work of cutting perfect pieces of bacon to your desired thickness, though you might also use a sharp knife for the task. Slightly freezing the bacon before slicing makes the job even easier.

Store your sliced bacon wrapped in freezer paper or vacuum-packed in your freezer for two to three months. If you make more than what you can gobble in that time, wrap and freeze in chunks instead, as it'll keep its fresh flavor longer if it's not sliced.

Curing and smoking bacon results in a delicious homemade food that will satisfy your taste buds, fill your belly and impress your friends. Give it a try; you won't regret it!

Ryan and Wendy Wilson live and work on an 80-acre farm in southwest Oregon, where they share his meat-cutting skills and her food-preserving prowess.

The desired thickness might vary depending on the intended use for your bacon.

Vacuum-sealed, labeled bacon is ready for the freezer.

MAPLE BACON 4/25/14

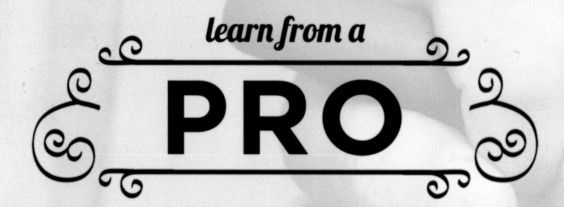

learn from a

PRO

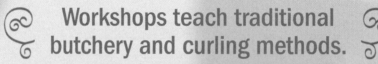

Workshops teach traditional butchery and curling methods.

BY AMY GRISAK

many bacon lovers take great pride in purchasing the highest-quality cured meats, yet anything we buy from conventional butchers pales in comparison to what the average farmer and his family ate just over a century ago. As more food lovers become aware of the culinary possibilities, many are taking knives into their own hands to learn the old ways of butchery and curing. A growing number of talented butchers and charcuterists offer hands-on workshops to teach anyone with a keen interest in learning how to create sublime meats.

A butcher wears protective gloves while cutting fresh pork.

AMMIT JACK /SHUTTERSTOCK

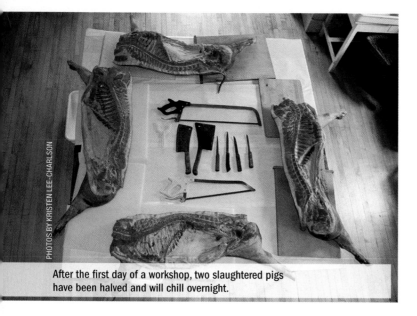

After the first day of a workshop, two slaughtered pigs have been halved and will chill overnight.

Sheard of Farmstead Meatsmith separates the meat from the bone in a hog's leg portion.

"There was no smoking involved in making the bacon."

"I really didn't know food could taste so good," says Brandon Sheard of Farmstead Meatsmith in Vashon, Washington, who teaches workshops on the peasant style of butchery and charcuterie. The "extravagant deliciousness," as Sheard describes his first taste of real bacon, hooked him. "I felt like I've been cheated my whole life."

Kristen Lee-Charlson, an heirloom food aficionado and founder of the Heirloom Project (a traditional foods group) in Huson, Montana, organized a workshop with Sheard to bring his experience to locals who wished to learn the craft. Lee-Charlson was beyond impressed with the quality of traditional bacon and cured meats.

"Think about the bacon you buy at the store. It's all wet," she points out. It's injected with flavoring and must be refrigerated to prevent spoilage.

This isn't the case with traditional bacon; it's a different entity. Sheard explains, "It's not a flavored piece of meat. It's preserved."

Using only a salt and sugar mixture, the goal is to remove the moisture from the meat. Every day, the meat is rinsed as moisture is released, and more of the salt/sugar mix is applied. Lee-

Charlson says the goal is complete rigidity as all the moisture is removed.

While bacon can be smoked, it doesn't have to be. "There was no smoking involved in making the bacon," Lee-Charlson says. "This is just the really pure, traditional style."

In France, she says, they sometimes hang it in chimneys as a way to flavor the meat, and there's nothing wrong with a cold-smoking step to add a dimension to the taste. It's not necessary for preservation, though.

What's truly amazing to most is that the final product doesn't have to be refrigerated. It's completely stable at room temperature. Sheard and his family hang their cured meats in their kitchen, making them accessible during meal preparation.

The result is bacon as you've never experienced. "The fat is just amazing," Lee-Charlson says. "It melts in your mouth. It's so satiating and satisfying." Thinly sliced bacon, fruit, cheese and a few nuts is a full meal in her book.

This return to a traditional style of butchering and charcuterie offers an answer to the desire for people to acquire sustainable, simple and delicious methods of putting meat on the table. "It's very easy to create bacon that tastes better than anything [people] will buy in this country," Sheard says.

He learned this art out of necessity while working for a small operation on Vashon Island where they prepared all of their own meats for the farmers market. With hogs and lambs hanging, and everyone else swamped with projects,

"In France, they like to say that every part of the pig is used except the oink." — Michael Ruhlman and Brian Polcyn, "Charcuterie" (W. W. Norton & Company)

Sheard demonstrates to a workshop participant how to remove the meat from the bone.

Side and back bacon (toward the top) and guanciale (pork jowl) have been rubbed down with an initial curing mix of salt and sugar.

"The fat is just amazing. It melts in your mouth."

Sheard took it upon himself to prepare the animals for the market.

"I was working from my knowledge of the finished cuts," he explains. With a knack for deconstruction, he took his first step in peasant-style butchery. From there, he dove into research to master the old ways of butchery and charcuterie.

After several years, he and his wife, Lauren, decided to offer personal abattoir and butchery services to small farmers and to provide educational workshops for people who eschew modern practices instead of traditional techniques, hand in hand with the quest for superior meats.

"It just so happens the most responsible way is the most delicious," Sheard says.

From Start to Finish

In his classes, eight people take knives in hand and learn the entire process. "It's all with a culinary focus and the goal of creating zero waste," he says. "It's my goal to show them it is simpler than it's portrayed. It's the realm of the sustainable family home. It's pure and basic."

The process begins with a calm, controlled death. Sheard says, "It's very common for people to be surprised at how artfully it can be done. No experience is necessary. Ignorance is preferred."

Typically when Sheard conducts a workshop, the first day is dedicated to the slaughter and initial steps, including scalding and scraping. The second day demonstrates how to create the cuts of meat that utilize every part of the animal. A third day teaches them the craft of creating cured meats and sausages.

Once completed, everyone should have a sound handle and increased confidence on completing the task at home, yet Sheard points out, "People have to learn how to cook again with the old cure. It's very rich."

Lee-Charlson says when you fry the traditionally cured bacon, the salt is very pronounced. It also imparts tremendous flavor when it's cubed and sautéed in dishes. When you consider cooking habits a century or more ago, it makes sense. They revered their animals because it took so much effort to raise and prepare them, so they didn't eat the large portions of meat that we do today.

In the quest for the ultimate bacon as well as other meats, consider taking the knife in your own hand to create a delicious nod to our agrarian roots. But be warned: Once you step into traditional realm, you'll never want to return to the bacon in the store.

> ## "It's all with a culinary focus and the goal of creating zero waste."

Amy Grisak (thebackyardbounty.com) appreciates the pastured hogs raised by friends near her home in Great Falls, Montana, and always looks for ways to work bacon into recipes for her family.

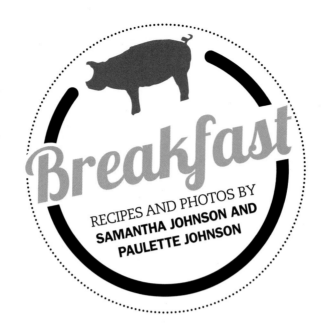

Breakfast

RECIPES AND PHOTOS BY SAMANTHA JOHNSON AND PAULETTE JOHNSON

Don't wake up on the wrong side of the bed — start the day off right by adding bacon to the most important meal of the day! Thanks to these delectable recipes, you'll have a hearty dose of bacon goodness to set the tone for a pig-ture-perfect day.

Cheery Bacon Breakfast Pizza

Why should you have to wait for lunch or dinner to enjoy a super-delicious pizza, when a breakfast pie brings you all that fun and flavor first thing in the morning? With eggs, onions, peppers and (of course!) bacon, these personal-size pizzas will start your morning with a smile.

Makes 4 to 6 pies

1 4-oz. package active-dry yeast
1 cup warm tap water (approximately 120 to 130 degrees Fahrenheit), divided
1 Tbsp. oil
2½ cups flour
1 tsp. sugar
1 tsp. salt
5 eggs
2 Tbsp. milk
salt and pepper to taste
2 Tbsp. butter
½ medium onion, chopped
½ red bell pepper, chopped
½ yellow bell pepper, chopped
½ green bell pepper, chopped
12 to 14 slices bacon, cooked and then cut in half
2 to 3 oz. Cheddar cheese, shredded (optional)
dried basil (optional but adds nice flavor)

1 Preheat the oven to 400 degrees F. In a small bowl, dissolve the yeast in ¼ cup warm water.

2 In a mixing bowl, add the dissolved yeast, remaining ¾ cup water, oil, flour, sugar and salt. Mix thoroughly, about 20 strokes or until the dough becomes a ball. Let the dough rest for 5 to 10 minutes.

3 Gently knead the dough on a lightly floured surface (about 2 minutes); then divide into equal pieces to make 4 to 6 crusts. Shape into disks with a thicker crust around the edges to contain the ingredients.

4 In a mixing bowl, whisk together the eggs, milk, salt and pepper.

5 In a skillet over medium-high heat, sauté the onion and peppers in butter until soft. Add the egg mixture, and cook until the eggs are no longer runny.

6 Layer 6 half-slices of bacon on each crust; spoon the egg/veggie mixture on top of the bacon on each pizza. Sprinkle the tops with dried basil, if desired.

7 Bake in the oven for 25 minutes. After 20 minutes of baking, lightly sprinkle Cheddar cheese over each pizza, if desired; then continue baking for 5 minutes.

Crumbled Bacon, Egg and Cheese Casserole

For an extraordinary weekend breakfast, whip up a batch of bacon, egg and cheese goodness. If you'd like to speed up the prep process, hard-boil your eggs in advance, and have them ready to go. Then sit back, relax, and enjoy the delight of this taste bud-pleasing casserole.

Serves 6

6 Tbsp. butter (¾ stick)
2 Tbsp. flour
1½ cups half-and-half
½ tsp. salt
¼ tsp. pepper
6 oz. Cheddar cheese, cut into small pieces
10 eggs — hardboiled, peeled and sliced lengthwise
12 strips of cooked bacon, crumbled
cracker crumbs (crumble about 20 to 25 Ritz-style crackers)

1 Preheat the oven to 350 degrees Fahrenheit.

2 In a medium saucepan, prepare the cheese sauce by melting the butter. Then add the flour slowly to prevent lumps from forming. Gradually add the half-and-half, and cook over low heat until it thickens a bit — about 10 minutes.

3 Add the salt, pepper and cheese. Stir until the cheese is fully melted; then remove the cheese sauce from the heat.

4 In a 9-by-9-inch pan, layer half of the eggs, followed by half of the crumbled bacon, then half of the cheese sauce. Repeat the layers again.

5 Sprinkle cracker crumbs over the top, and bake for 40 minutes. Serve immediately.

Apple-maple-bacon Muffins

In the mood for pancakes and bacon but don't have time to cook up a big breakfast? Toss together a batch of these extra-special pancake-inspired muffins, and then drizzle the maple syrup-infused glaze over the tops. You can store these in the fridge and have them at your fingertips for busy mornings when you still want a yummy treat.

Makes 18 to 24 muffins

Muffins
2 cups all-purpose flour
3 Tbsp. sugar
2 tsp. baking powder
½ tsp. salt
½ tsp. cinnamon
¼ tsp. nutmeg
2 eggs
3 Tbsp. vegetable oil
1¾ cups milk
2 Tbsp. maple syrup
1 apple, peeled and grated (such as Braeburn)
12 slices bacon, cooked and crumbled

Glaze
3 Tbsp. butter
1½ cups powdered sugar
1 tsp. vanilla
1 Tbsp. maple syrup
2 Tbsp. water

1 Preheat the oven to 375 degrees Fahrenheit.

2 In a mixing bowl, combine the dry ingredients: flour, sugar, baking powder, salt, cinnamon and nutmeg. In a separate bowl, combine the eggs, vegetable oil, milk and maple syrup.

3 Add the wet ingredients to the dry ingredients, and mix lightly. Then fold in the apple and bacon bits.

4 Lightly grease or spray a 12-cup muffin tin; fill each cup ⅔ full with batter. Bake for 17 to 20 minutes.

5 To prepare the glaze: In a saucepan, heat all of the ingredients until combined and smooth, stirring constantly. Drizzle over the baked muffins after removing them from the tin. Sprinkle the tops with additional crumbled bacon if desired.

6 Store unglazed, leftover muffins in the refrigerator for 3 days at most. They also can be frozen and reheated.

Samantha Johnson is the author of several books, including "The Beginner's Guide to Vegetable Gardening" (Voyageur Press). Paulette Johnson, a professional photographer and writer, enjoys cooking and gardening.

RECIPES BY
JENNIFER MACKENZIE
PHOTOS BY
PATRICIA LEHNHARDT

Bacon makes classic quick breads taste even better with the splash of smoky, salty flavor. When buying bacon to use in these recipes, choose a high-quality, flavorful bacon; an overly salty or high-fat, low-yield bacon (one pumped with a lot of water) won't give the desired, balanced flavor to your baked goods. So, cook up a big batch of bacon, and save some in the fridge or freezer to have at the ready to perk up your quick breads.

Marmalade Bacon Loaf

This might seem like an unusual combination, but the tangy, bitter marmalade; sweet loaf; and smoky, salty bacon combine for a delightful treat with a cup of coffee or tea. Leftovers make fantastic French toast or can be buttered and grilled and then served with ice cream for a decadent dessert.

Makes 1 loaf of about 12 slices

2¼ cups all-purpose flour
2 tsp. baking powder
½ tsp. baking soda
½ tsp. salt
½ cup good-quality orange marmalade
2 eggs
½ cup granulated sugar
½ cup butter, melted
1 cup plain yogurt (not fat-free)
1 tsp. vanilla extract
11 slices or ⅔ cup finely chopped, crisply cooked bacon

1 Preheat oven to 350 degrees Fahrenheit. Butter a 9-by-5-inch metal loaf pan, or line it with parchment paper.

2 In a large bowl, whisk together the flour, baking powder, baking soda and salt. Set aside.

3 Warm the marmalade slightly in a saucepan or microwave until softened. Press through a sieve, reserving jelly in a bowl. Finely chop rind pieces, and stir into jelly.

4 Add eggs and sugar to marmalade; whisk until blended. Whisk in butter, yogurt and vanilla until blended. Stir in bacon. Pour over dry ingredients, and stir until moistened.

5 Spread batter into the prepared pan, smoothing the top. Bake for 50 minutes or until a tester inserted in the center comes out clean.

6 Let cool in the pan on a wire rack for 20 minutes; then remove from the pan, and let cool completely on the rack. Store the loaf well-wrapped at room temperature for up to 2 days, or freeze for up to 2 months.

The number
of slices you use
might vary because
of your bacon's
thickness and quality
and its shrinkage
while being
cooked.

Chive & Bacon Cornbread

This classic cornbread offers an added burst of bacon to serve with your favorite soup, chili or stew. Toasted slices, topped with a zippy cheese, make for a great lunch or snack.

If you don't have a cast-iron skillet, you can use a 9-inch round or square metal cake pan. Just cook the bacon in a separate skillet, and skip heating the pan in the oven. Brush the cake pan with bacon fat or butter, and increase the baking time to 30 minutes.

Makes 6 to 8 pieces

1 cup all-purpose flour
1 cup yellow cornmeal, preferably stone-ground
2 tsp. baking powder
½ tsp. salt
½ tsp. freshly ground black pepper
¼ tsp. baking soda
2 eggs
2 Tbsp. granulated sugar
1¼ cups buttermilk
½ cup mild olive oil or melted butter
6 slices high-quality side bacon, chopped
¼ cup finely chopped fresh chives or scallions

1 Preheat oven to 400 degrees Fahrenheit. In a large bowl, whisk together flour, cornmeal, baking powder, salt, pepper and baking soda. In another bowl, whisk together eggs, sugar, buttermilk and oil until blended.

2 Cook bacon in a deep, 8- to 9-inch cast-iron skillet, stirring, for 5 minutes or until crisp. Transfer bacon to a paper towel-lined plate to drain.

3 Pour off the bacon fat, leaving just a thin coating of fat in the pan. (Discard any remaining fat, or reserve for another use.) Brush fat over the skillet's bottom and sides evenly. Place the skillet in the oven while mixing batter.

4 Pour the buttermilk mixture over dry ingredients, and sprinkle with bacon and chives. Stir just until moistened.

5 Pour the batter into the hot skillet. Bake for 20 to 25 minutes or until golden around the edges and a tester inserted in the center comes out clean.

6 Let cool in the pan on a wire rack for 10 minutes. Serve hot, warm or at room temperature. This is best served the day it's baked. Leftovers can be wrapped and stored at room temperature for up to 2 days and reheated or toasted before serving.

Bacon-studded Biscuit Cinnamon Rolls

What could be better than easy-to-make, sweetly spiced, buttery cinnamon rolls? Cinnamon rolls with bacon in them! This biscuit dough requires just a quick mix and no rising, so you can make up a batch for breakfast in just a few minutes. While they bake, put the coffee on, cut up some fruit, and get ready to fend off your family who won't be able to resist these sweet treats. They are best the day they're made, but you can hold off on icing them, wrap them well for up to a day, and reheat the rolls wrapped in foil at 350 degrees Fahrenheit for 15 minutes.

Makes 8 rolls

Filling
¼ cup butter, softened
½ cup packed brown sugar
2 tsp. ground cinnamon
½ tsp. ground ginger (optional)
8 slices or ½ cup crumbled, crisply cooked bacon

Dough
2⅓ cups all-purpose flour
3 Tbsp. packed brown sugar
1 Tbsp. baking powder
1 tsp. baking soda
½ tsp. ground cinnamon
¼ tsp. salt
½ cup cold butter, cut into cubes
1 cup buttermilk

Icing
1 to 2 Tbsp. buttermilk
½ cup confectioners' sugar

1 Preheat oven to 425 degrees F. Generously butter a 9-inch round, metal cake pan.

2 In a bowl, mash together butter, brown sugar, cinnamon and ginger (if using). Set aside.

3 In another bowl, combine the flour, sugar, baking powder, baking soda, cinnamon and salt. Cut in the butter with a pastry blender until coarse crumbs form (or pulse in a food processor and then transfer to a bowl). Drizzle buttermilk over the mixture, and stir with a fork until a soft dough forms.

4 Gather with your hands, and transfer the dough to a lightly floured surface. Gently knead two or three times or just until smooth.

5 With a floured rolling pin, roll out to a 14-by-10-inch rectangle. Spread with filling, leaving a 1-inch border along one long edge. Sprinkle evenly with bacon.

6 Starting at the dough's long edge opposite the plain border, gently roll up jelly-roll style. With a serrated knife, cut crosswise into 8 slices. Arrange slices, cut side down, in the prepared pan.

7 Bake for 25 to 30 minutes or until puffed and browned and a tester inserted in between center rolls comes out clean. Let cool for 15 minutes to serve hot, or let cool completely.

8 In a small bowl, stir 1 Tbsp. of buttermilk into confectioners' sugar; gradually stir in just enough of the remaining buttermilk to make a thick consistency. Unmold rolls from pan, if desired, and then drizzle the icing over cinnamon rolls just before serving.

Bacon Day is celebrated each year on the Saturday before Labor Day.

Bacon & Sweet Pepper Cheese Muffins

Whether you enjoy these for a breakfast on-the-go, packed for lunch or as an accompaniment to a bowl of soup or salad, you can't go wrong with these savory muffins. For added punch, add half of a minced jalapeño pepper, ½ tsp. smoked paprika and/or ¾ cup roasted or grilled corn kernels with the red pepper.

Makes 12 muffins

1¼ cups all-purpose flour
1 cup whole wheat flour
1 Tbsp. baking powder
½ tsp. freshly ground black pepper
¼ tsp. salt
1 cup shredded sharp Cheddar cheese
8 slices or ½ cup chopped crisply cooked bacon
1 egg
2 Tbsp. granulated sugar
1 cup milk
½ cup plain yogurt
¼ cup vegetable oil or melted butter
¾ cup diced red bell pepper

1 Preheat oven to 375 degrees Fahrenheit. Butter or spray a 12-cup muffin pan.

2 In a large bowl, whisk together the flours, baking powder, pepper and salt. Stir in cheese and bacon.

3 In another bowl, whisk together egg, sugar, milk, yogurt and oil until blended. Pour over dry ingredients, and sprinkle with red peppers. Stir just until moistened.

4 Divide the batter equally into the pan. Bake for 20 minutes or until the tops spring back when lightly touched.

5 Let cool in the pan on a wire rack for 10 minutes; then transfer muffins to the rack to cool. Serve warm or at room temperature. Store in an airtight container for up to 1 day, or freeze for up to 1 month.

A professional home economist, Jennifer MacKenzie (jennifermackenzie.net) owns FoodWorx and creates cookbooks.

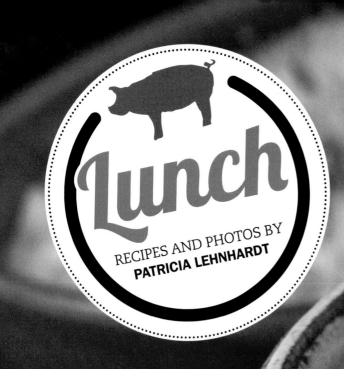

Lunch

RECIPES AND PHOTOS BY
PATRICIA LEHNHARDT

In salads, sandwiches and good old macaroni and cheese, bacon makes lunchtime extra special. It pairs well with cheese or tomatoes or beef or chicken or … Wait! What does bacon not go with?

Bacon Mac and Cheese

Any style of short pasta will work in this dish, but I have it on good authority (i.e., my granddaughter) there is really only one: "You know, the ones that are smiley faces, and when you turn them upside-down, they are sad faces... that kind." Kids really know best when it comes to mac and cheese!

Serves 4

1 Tbsp. salt
1 cup elbow macaroni
2 cups broccoli florets
½ lb. bacon, cut into ½-inch dice (8 slices)
3 Tbsp. all-purpose flour
1 cup chicken broth
1 cup heavy cream
freshly ground black pepper to taste
¼ tsp. freshly ground nutmeg
6 oz. sharp Cheddar cheese, grated (3 cups)
4 oz. feta cheese, grated (1½ cups)
¼ cup grated Parmesan cheese

1   Bring a large pot of water to a boil. Add salt and macaroni. Cook at a rolling boil for 6 to 7 minutes, until just tender.

2   Add the broccoli, and cook 1 minute. Drain.

3   In a large skillet, fry the bacon over medium heat until crisp and the fat is rendered. Remove the bacon with a slotted spoon, and drain on paper towels.

4   Pour out all but 3 Tbsp. bacon fat from the pan, and whisk in the flour. Whisking constantly, cook for 1 minute.

5   Add the broth and cream. Cook, whisking constantly until thickened and free of lumps for 2 minutes.

6   Remove from the heat, and whisk in the pepper, nutmeg, Cheddar and feta, stirring until the cheeses melt. The feta will not melt completely. Fold in the macaroni, broccoli and bacon.

7   Preheat oven broiler to high. Divide the mixture into 4 1½-cup casserole dishes. Sprinkle each one with 1 Tbsp. Parmesan cheese.

8   Broil for 5 minutes until golden-brown and bubbly. Let cool for 5 to 10 minutes before serving.

Beef and Bacon Burgers or Meatball Subs

Finding the perfect blend of bacon and beef is a matter of experimentation. A 50/50 ratio or even 100 percent bacon is possible. This one is a bit conservative with a 25/75 percent ratio. The bacon adds a smoky quality to the burger without overwhelming it. The meatball recipe offers another option, and the spicy ketchup tops it off perfectly.

Serves 4

¾ lb. ground beef
¼ lb. ground bacon* (4 thick-cut strips)
salt and pepper to taste

* To grind bacon: Cut uncooked bacon into ½-inch pieces, and freeze for 20 minutes. Put through a meat grinder or pulse in a food processor until you see the desired texture.

Burgers

1 In a large mixing bowl, blend the beef and bacon by hand, and form into 4 patties. Season with salt and pepper.

2 Grill or pan-fry until desired doneness — about 4 minutes per side for medium.

3 Serve on buns with spicy ketchup and desired garnishes.

Meatball Subs

1 lb. beef/bacon blend
½ cup diced onion
½ cup diced red bell pepper
½ cup breadcrumbs
1 egg
2 Tbsp. chopped parsley

1 In a medium bowl, combine the meat, onion, bell pepper, breadcrumbs, egg and parsley. Form into 16 meatballs.

2 In a skillet, fry until browned on all sides. Add the spicy ketchup, and cook for 3 minutes to glaze the meatballs.

Suggested serving: on hoagie buns with lettuce, sliced tomatoes and sliced cucumber.

Spicy Ketchup

1 Tbsp. bacon fat
1 shallot, minced (3 Tbsp.)
1 clove garlic, minced
¼ tsp. chipotle chili powder
¾ cup ketchup

1 In a small saucepan, melt the bacon fat. Add the shallot and garlic, and sauté until softened.

2 Add the chipotle powder and ketchup, and simmer for 3 to 4 minutes.

Ramp Up the BLT

MAYONNAISE SUBSTITUTES

Bacon Aioli: makes ½ cup
1 fresh egg yolk
2 Tbsp. fresh lemon juice
2 cloves garlic
¼ cup melted bacon fat
¼ cup olive oil
salt and pepper to taste

1 In a blender, combine the egg yolk, lemon juice and garlic. Process until smooth.

2 In a measuring cup, combine the bacon fat and olive oil. Remove the cap on the lid of the blender and, with the machine running, slowly pour the fat into the egg mixture. The mayonnaise will thicken as it emulsifies. Add seasonings if desired.

Dressed-up Mayo: makes ½ cup
¼ cup sun-dried tomato pesto or basil pesto
¼ cup mayonnaise

Stir together in a small bowl.

Tomatoes
heirloom tomatoes of all colors, fried green tomatoes, thinly sliced Roma tomatoes, marinated tomatoes with vinaigrette and fresh minced herbs

When tomatoes are not in season, the best-tasting tomatoes available are cherry tomatoes (red or yellow). Mixed in a salad and piled high on crispy waffles, they will give you the flavor of summer any time of year.

Bread choices
white sourdough, seedy whole wheat, crispy thin waffles, grilled garlic bread, French toast, spinach or whole-wheat wraps, croissants, corn or flour tortillas, rice paper wraps

Lettuce alternatives
arugula, basil, spinach

Add-ins
avocado slices, cheese of any kind, guacamole, fried egg, thinly sliced cucumber, thinly sliced radishes, marinated artichokes

BLT

Bacon, lettuce and tomato: the simplest of recipes. Five ingredients are key to the perfect balance of smoky, sweet, acid, crunch and salt. Some say "Don't mess with perfection," while others argue "More is better." You be the judge — classic or ramped up.

Classic Basics

2 pieces of the best white bread you can find, toasted
4 strips of your favorite bacon, fried crisp
3 slices of the ripest, in-season tomatoes
2 leaves of mild crunchy lettuce: iceberg, leaf or romaine
2 Tbsp. mayonnaise

Toast the bread and fry the bacon right before assembling. Room-temperature tomatoes and chilled lettuce and mayonnaise offer the best combination of warm, cold and crunchy texture.

BLT Salad on Crispy Waffles

Serves 4

4 strips bacon, fried crisp and broken into ½-inch pieces
1 cup quartered cherry tomatoes
1 cup shredded romaine lettuce
2 Tbsp. mayonnaise
4 thin waffles, toasted

Mix the bacon, tomatoes, lettuce and mayonnaise. Divide between 2 waffles, and top with the other 2.

Cheddar, Bacon and Apple Panini

Tangy, sharp Cheddar; sweet apples; and smoky, salty bacon form the perfect combination for a grilled cheese sandwich special enough for company. This is everyone's favorite and pairs well with the anticipated bowl of tomato soup.

Makes 4 sandwiches

8 strips bacon
2 garlic cloves, minced
1 small onion, diced (¾ cup)
1 large Granny Smith apple, peeled and diced
¼ cup brown sugar
¼ cup water
½ tsp. ground cinnamon
½ tsp. mild curry powder
pinch of red pepper flakes
8 slices bread
2 Tbsp. bacon grease
1½ cups grated sharp Cheddar cheese

1 In a large skillet, fry the bacon until crisp. Drain on paper towels. Break in half.

2 Drain all but 1 Tbsp. fat from the pan, and add the garlic and onions. Sauté until tender and starting to brown.

3 Add the apple, and cook until beginning to brown on the edges. Add the sugar, water, cinnamon, curry powder and red pepper flakes.

4 Cover and simmer until the apple is tender, about 6 to 8 minutes, stirring occasionally. Uncover, and continue to cook until the sauce has thickened. Let cool.

5 Spread the bread with bacon fat on one side only. Build a sandwich with a slice of bread, bacon fat down, 3 Tbsp. cheese, a quarter of the apple mixture, 4 half strips of bacon, 3 Tbsp. cheese and the other slice of bread with the bacon-fat side up. Repeat to make 3 more sandwiches.

6 Bake in a panini grill, or fry in a large skillet on both sides until the cheese melts and the bread is golden-brown.

> *The word "bacon" comes from the German word bacho, which means buttocks.*

Chicken Salad with Bacon

This is the perfect combination to dress up chicken salad. The lettuce cups create an individual component that sets it apart and adds a fresh crunch to the flavorful bacon.

Serves 4

½ lb. bacon (8 strips)
1 large skinless, boneless chicken breast (½ lb.)
salt and pepper to taste
3 scallions, white and light green parts, thinly sliced
1 clove garlic, minced
2 Tbsp. lemon juice
3 Tbsp. mayonnaise
1 large tomato, cut into ½-inch cubes
1 avocado, cut into ½-inch cubes
1 cup thinly sliced celery
1 Tbsp. capers
4 lettuce cups from a head of butter crunch lettuce
1 Tbsp. thinly sliced scallion greens for garnish, if desired

1 In a large skillet, fry the bacon until crisp.

2 Cut the chicken in half horizontally, so each piece is about ½ inch thick. Season both sides with salt and pepper.

3 When the bacon is crisp, remove it from the pan, and drain on paper towels. Fry the chicken in the skillet with the bacon fat, 4 to 5 minutes per side, until browned and cooked through. Transfer the chicken to a cutting board to rest.

4 Pour out all but 4 Tbsp. fat. Add the scallions and garlic, and sauté for 1 minute until softened.

5 Add the lemon juice, and scrape up the browned bits from the bottom of the pan. Remove from the heat, and whisk in the mayonnaise until smooth.

6 Cut the bacon and chicken into ½-inch pieces. In a large bowl, combine them with the tomato, avocado, celery and capers. Add the mayonnaise mixture, and gently fold together. Season to taste with salt and pepper.

7 Arrange a cup of salad in each lettuce cup, and sprinkle with scallion greens.

Patricia Lehnhardt revels in all things bacon and, while working on recipes and photos for this magazine, visited different grocery stores to avoid depleting their inventories all at once. She shares more recipes at www.thetraveling table.com

Appetizers

RECIPES AND PHOTOS BY
FIONA GREEN

*Bacon helps you start any soirée — small or large —
with unexpected pizzazz. Whether the meat plays a supporting
role in cheese balls or has a star turn in a candied
version, it'll tickle your guests' tastebuds.*

Mini Bacon, Olive and Jalapeño Cheese Balls

These delicious cheese balls look like luxury chocolate truffles and make an attractive addition to any dinner. While this recipe uses ground pecans, you can roll the cheese balls in sesame seeds, crushed pistachios or sliced almonds, too. They are delicious served on their own or with crackers and a tangy chutney.

Makes 16 balls

8 slices bacon
1 cup whole pecans
8 oz. cream cheese or goat cheese
1 cup grated, aged/mature Cheddar cheese
1 jalapeño pepper, finely chopped
¼ cup black olives (about 10)
1 tsp. Worcestershire sauce
1 tsp. lime juice
2 Tbsp. finely chopped parsley
½ tsp. mesquite flavoring
salt and pepper to taste
16 pretzel sticks

1 Preheat the oven to 350 degrees Fahrenheit. Grill or fry the bacon until crispy. Remove from heat, crumble into small pieces, and set aside.

2 Evenly scatter the pecans on a baking tray. Bake in the oven for about 5 minutes, turning halfway through cooking.

3 Remove the nuts from the oven, and let them cool. Grind the oats in a coffee grinder, or crush them with a rolling pin. Set aside in a small bowl.

4 In a large bowl, combine the cheeses, bacon, jalapeño pepper, olives, Worcestershire sauce, lime juice, parsley and seasonings. Mix the ingredients well; then form 16 individual balls.

5 Roll each ball in pecans, and refrigerate for 1 hour to overnight. When ready to serve, insert a pretzel stick into each ball, arrange on a serving tray, and prepare to wow your guests.

The number of slices you use might vary because of your bacon's thickness and quality and its shrinkage while being cooked.

Bacon and Mango Spring Rolls With Peanut Sauce

There is nothing more delicious than a fresh spring roll. Perfect as a light lunch or mid-afternoon snack, these irresistible parcels are packed with healthy goodness and surprisingly easy to make after some practice. When served with a creamy peanut sauce or a hot chili sauce, they are sure to be a crowd pleaser.

Makes 6 rolls

½ cup uncooked rice noodles
1 ripe mango, julienned
1 romaine lettuce heart, chopped
½ red pepper, julienned

6 slices Canadian bacon (about 1 cup), cut into thin slices
6 9-inch round rice wrappers
⅓ cup fresh mint (about 24 leaves)

1 In a large pot, place the rice noodles in boiling water, and cook for about 6 minutes or until soft. Remove from the heat. Place in a colander, rinse with cold water, and drain. Set aside the noodles.

2 Dip the rice wrappers, one by one, very briefly into lukewarm water, and then lay flat on a work surface. Do not soak them for too long, or they

Peanut Dipping Sauce

The sauce can be made ahead of time and refrigerated until ready to use.

¾ cup crunchy peanut butter
1½ cup coconut milk
¼ cup lime juice
2 Tbsp. soy sauce
2 tsp. molasses
1 tsp. ginger
4 garlic cloves, minced
¼ cup heavy cream
¼ cup chicken broth
pinch of paprika
3 Tbsp. maple syrup
1 tsp. fresh cilantro

1 In a saucepan, mix the peanut butter, coconut milk, lime juice, soy sauce, molasses, ginger and garlic. Cook over moderate heat, stirring occasionally.

2 When the sauce has a creamy consistency, transfer to a blender. Purée for 10 seconds; then add cream, chicken broth and paprika. Purée for 10 seconds.

3 Allow to cool; then pour into a bowl, and stir in maple syrup. Refrigerate overnight; the sauce will thicken. Before serving, sprinkle cilantro on the sauce.

will lose their shape and become difficult to handle. They will soften while you work.

3 Take a handful of noodles, fruit, vegetables, bacon and mint, and place in a small pile on one side of the wrapper. Fold over the edge closest to the ingredients to cover them, and then fold in the ends to hold everything in place.

4 Continue to roll the wrapper tightly around the ingredients until you have formed a roll. Practice makes perfect with spring rolls, but once you have mastered the art, they can be made in less time that it takes to prepare a sandwich.

Crustless Quiches with Bacon and Sun-dried Tomatoes

In my world, real men like quiche (and cats). In this recipe, juicy sun-dried tomatoes, hickory-smoked bacon and creamy goat cheese combine to offer a taste sensation that proves difficult to resist. Instead of using pastry, I have used a light coating of breadcrumbs to let the tasty filling take center stage.

This recipe uses mini muffin cups and creates 30 tasty, one-bite quiches. If you prefer to use regular-size muffin cups, the recipe will make 16 quiches with 5 extra minutes of cooking time.

Makes 30 mini quiches

8 slices bacon to make 1 cup crumbled bits
15 tsp. Italian-style breadcrumbs
8 eggs
1½ cups heavy whipping cream
1 cup crumbled goat cheese
½ cup sun-dried tomatoes, finely chopped
1 tsp. chipotle seasoning
salt and pepper to taste

1 Preheat the oven to 350 degrees Fahrenheit. Cook the bacon until crispy. Remove from heat, crumble into small pieces, and set aside.

2 Spray the muffin cups with cooking spray. Place about ½ teaspoon of breadcrumbs in each muffin cup. Move the pan and tap it to lightly coat the sides of each muffin cup.

3 In a large bowl, beat the eggs with the cream. Add the goat cheese, bacon, sun-dried tomatoes and seasonings, and mix well.

4 Carefully spoon the filling into cups, and bake for about 15 minutes. When the quiches are ready, a toothpick inserted into the center should come out clean. Remove from the oven, and serve warm.

Bacon and Brie Phyllo Parcels

The ultimate comfort snack, these crispy bites will steal the show at any party. Your heart will skip a beat as you bite into the flaky, buttery pastry and savor the flavor of bacon and melted brie. These appetizers are delicious on their own or with apricot jelly.

Makes 12 parcels

12 slices bacon
10 oz. brie
4 green onions
6 13-by-17-inch phyllo sheets
⅓ cup melted butter
2 Tbsp. sesame seeds and 2 Tbsp. chopped parsley
  to garnish

1 Preheat oven to 350 degrees Fahrenheit. Cook the bacon until crisp. Remove from heat, drain, and crumble into small pieces.

2 Cut brie into 1-inch cubes, and slice the green onions very thinly.

3 Roll out a sheet of phyllo. Dab melted butter evenly over the sheet with a pastry brush. Lay a second sheet on top of the first layer, and repeat with butter. Add a third layer.

4 Cut phyllo layers into 6 squares. In the center of each square, place the bacon, brie and chopped onions.

5 Fold the top 2 sheets of each phyllo dough square over the filling. Then gather the third sheet and shape it to form a decorative parcel. If desired, sprinkle the sesame seeds on top for decoration.

6 Repeat the process with the remaining phyllo sheets. Place parcels on a baking tray, and bake in the oven for about 12 minutes or until golden-brown.

7 Before serving, let parcels cool for 3 to 5 minutes, and sprinkle them with parsley.

Candied Bacon with Cardamom

This treat satisfies both your sweet tooth and your desire for something savory. Rose water and a light sprinkling of cardamom add an unexpected and delightful flavor, while multicolored peppercorns contribute a little spice to an already heavenly concoction. As an alternative to peppercorns, you can add crushed pistachios.

Candied bacon is delicious on its own or as an inspired addition to cocktails. It's also addictive, so make plenty to keep everyone happy!

Makes 16 pieces

16 slices bacon
8 Tbsp. maple syrup
4 tsp. rose water
1 cup brown sugar
1 Tbsp. ground cardamom
⅓ cup black and pink peppercorns or crushed pistachios

1 Preheat oven to 350 degrees Fahrenheit. In a small bowl, mix the maple syrup and rose water.

2 Place a sheet of aluminum foil on a baking tray; use a tray with sides to prevent spillage. This will make it easier to clean up.

3 Evenly lay out bacon strips on foil, and bake in the oven for about 8 minutes. Remove from the oven, baste both sides with maple syrup mix, and dip in brown sugar.

4 Return to the oven, and bake for 8 to 12 minutes depending on the thickness of the bacon. Keep checking on the bacon to make sure it does not burn.

5 Remove the bacon from the oven, and place strips on a sheet of parchment paper. Sprinkle a pinch of cardamom and peppercorns or pistachios onto each strip, and allow to cool.

When she's not rescuing homeless animals or running half marathons, Fiona Green can be found in her kitchen, concocting delicious dishes like the ones seen in this magazine.

Main Dishes

RECIPES AND PHOTOS BY
PATRICIA LEHNHARDT

Bacon can be the star of the dish, as in a savory bread pudding, or simply enhance other meats like salmon, turkey and beef. The aroma draws you in and the crispy texture delights your mouth, but it's that rich, smoky flavor that really makes a dish special.

Bacon and Kale Savory Bread Pudding

A big salad is all you need to complete dinner with this filling casserole. Best made a day ahead, it's ready to put in the oven after a long day at work or errands — comfort food at its best.

Serves 4 to 6

6 bacon strips
1 medium onion, diced (1 cup)
½ red bell pepper, diced (½ cup)
8 oz. cremini mushrooms, cut in half and sliced
 (2 cups)
1 small bunch curly kale, stemmed and chopped
 (4 cups, lightly packed)
1 cup vegetable stock
4 eggs
1 cup milk
½ cup heavy cream
1 tsp. dried thyme
½ tsp. chipotle chili powder
1 tsp. smoked paprika
1 small loaf French bread, cut into ½-inch cubes
 (5 to 6 cups, lightly packed)
5 oz. blue cheese, crumbled (1 cup)

1 In a large skillet, fry the bacon until crisp. Drain on paper towels, and chop into bits.

2 Pour out all but 1 Tbsp. of the bacon fat. Add the onion, bell pepper and mushrooms to the pan. Sauté until soft and the onions are translucent.

3 Add the kale and stock. Cover and simmer for 15 minutes, until tender.

4 Uncover the skillet, and remove from the heat, letting it cool for 10 minutes.

5 In a large bowl, beat together the eggs, milk, cream, thyme, chipotle powder and smoked paprika. Add the vegetables, bacon, bread cubes and cheese.

6 Butter a 1½-quart casserole dish, and spoon the bread mixture into it. Cover with plastic wrap, and refrigerate overnight or up to 2 days.

7 Preheat the oven to 350 degrees Fahrenheit. Bake for 1 hour, until set and crusty brown on the top. Let rest for 15 minutes before serving.

Bacon- and Spinach-stuffed Pork Tenderloin

This dish includes a beautiful presentation with Greek-style spinach stuffing — enhanced with bacon, of course!

Serves 6 to 8

6 bacon strips
1 medium onion, diced (1 cup)
1 tsp. dried oregano
salt and pepper to taste
5 oz. baby spinach (3 cups, lightly packed)
1 egg
4 oz. feta cheese (1½ cups crumbled)
1 cup bread crumbs
2 pork tenderloins (2½ lbs.)
3 garlic cloves, minced
½ cup dry white wine
1 cup heavy cream

1   In a large skillet, cook the bacon until crisp. Drain the bacon on paper towels, and pour off all but 1 Tbsp. of the fat, reserving the rest for later.

2   Place the onion in the pan to sauté until soft and translucent. Season with oregano, salt and pepper.

3   Add the spinach, and cook until wilted — about 2 minutes. Set aside to cool for 10 minutes. Add the egg, feta and breadcrumbs, and mix thoroughly.

4   Preheat the oven to 400 degrees Fahrenheit. Trim the pork tenderloins of excess fat and silver skin.

5   Butterfly the meat by cutting it in half horizontally on the long edge to within ½ inch of the other side. Open like a book, and place between 2 sheets of parchment paper.

6   Pound with a meat mallet until the pork is about ½ inch thick. Remove the top sheet of parchment, and spread half of the spinach mixture over the surface of the meat.

7   Roll up, starting with a long side. Tie in several places with kitchen twine to hold the roll together. Repeat with the other tenderloin.

8   Add the reserved bacon fat to the skillet. Heat until the fat shimmers, and place the tenderloin rolls in the pan.

9   Brown on all sides, turning every few minutes — about 8 minutes total. Place in the oven, and roast until the internal temperature reaches 145 degrees F — about 30 minutes. Place the meat on a cutting board, and cover loosely with foil to rest.

10   Put the pan on the stove over medium-high heat. Add minced garlic, and sauté for 30 seconds. Add the white wine, scraping up all of the browned bits.

11   When the wine is reduced by half, add the heavy cream. Continue to cook on high heat, whisking occasionally until the sauce is thickened — 4 to 5 minutes. Season with salt and pepper.

12   Cut the tenderloin into ½-inch slices, and serve with garlic cream sauce.

Bolognese with a Hint of Bacon

Indistinguishable at first glance, the bacon adds just that certain touch that puts this Bolognese over the top. A slight smokiness on your palate gives it away.

Makes about 12 cups sauce, enough to serve 12 to 16 over pasta

3 Tbsp. olive oil
1 large carrot, finely diced (½ cup)
1 medium onion, diced (1 cup)
1 celery stalk, finely diced (½ cup)
2 garlic cloves, minced
¼ lb. bacon (4 strips), very finely chopped
1 large pork chop, bone-in
1 lb. ground beef
1 tsp. dried thyme
1 tsp. dried oregano
1 tsp. dried sage
1 large bay leaf
1 tsp. salt
1 large can peeled whole tomatoes (28 oz.)
2 small cans tomato paste (12 oz. total)
1 cup beef stock
½ cup dry red wine
½ cup heavy cream
¼ cup chopped fresh basil

1. In a large pot, heat the oil. Add the carrot, onion, celery and garlic. Sauté over medium heat until softened.

2. Raise the heat to high, and add the bacon, pork chop and ground beef. Break up the beef, and cook until it begins to brown.

3. Add the thyme, oregano, sage, bay leaf, salt, tomatoes, tomato paste, stock and wine. Break up the tomatoes with a spoon.

4. Bring to a boil, lower the heat, and cover. Simmer for about 2 hours, adding more stock if it becomes dry, stirring occasionally.

5. When the pork chop is very tender, remove from the pot and shred the meat, discarding the bones. Retrieve and discard the bay leaf.

6. Return the pork to the sauce, and add the cream. Cover and simmer for 30 minutes. Turn off the heat, and stir in the basil.

7. Serve over pasta, and garnish with Parmesan cheese. This sauce freezes well for 4 to 6 months.

Bacon-wrapped Salmon Pinwheels with Parsley Sauce

These pinwheels are perfect for a buffet, served on a bed of greens with a bowl of sauce on the side. The bacon adds richness to the salmon and helps to hold the rolls together.

Serves 4

2 garlic cloves
½ tsp. salt
1 cup coarsely chopped parsley, loosely packed
¼ cup olive oil
1 tsp. lemon zest
6 Tbsp. mayonnaise
8 thin-cut bacon strips
1 lb. salmon filet, cut into 8 1-inch slices, skinned

1 In a small food processor, chop the garlic. Add the salt and parsley, and process until finely ground. Drizzle in the oil, and process until smooth.

2 In a small bowl, mix 2 Tbsp. of the parsley oil with the lemon zest and mayonnaise. Set aside for serving. Reserve the remaining parsley oil to spread onto the salmon.

3 In a large skillet, cook the bacon until almost crisp but still pliable. Drain the bacon on paper towels, and allow to cool while preparing the salmon. Drain all but 1 Tbsp. bacon fat from the skillet.

4 Lay the salmon filets with the skinned side up on the work surface, and spread a heaping teaspoon of parsley oil on top. Roll up the filet, starting at the thickest end. Wrap a piece of cooked bacon around the roll, and secure with toothpicks.

5 Cook the salmon in the skillet. Cook for 4 minutes on each side or until it reaches the desired doneness. Remove the toothpicks, and serve with the parsley sauce.

Actor Kevin Bacon was the inspiration for a sculpture of his face made out of bacon bits. A Bacon Kevin Bacon was created by artist Mike Lahue and commissioned by Justin Esch and Dave Lefkow, owners of Seattle's J&D's Foods (company motto: "Everything should taste like bacon"). The bacon Bacon bust was auctioned on eBay in 2010 with proceeds going to a charity inspired by Lefkow's young daughter, who battled acute lymphoblastic leukemia.

Bacon-wrapped Turkey Roast

This is an adaptation of a perfect Christmas dinner for any time of year. Turkey tenderloins should be readily available at your local grocery store, and the beautiful woven bacon lures you into the moist turkey goodness. Leftovers can find their way thinly sliced in a sandwich or topping a green salad.

Serves 6 to 8

2 Tbsp. butter
1 large leek, diced (1½ cups)
salt and pepper to taste
1 tsp. dried sage
2 turkey breast tenderloins
8 bacon strips

1 Preheat the oven to 350 degrees Fahrenheit.

2 In a medium skillet, melt the butter, and add the leek. Sauté until softened — about 6 to 8 minutes. Season with salt, pepper and sage. Set aside to cool.

3 Butterfly each tenderloin by cutting it horizontally in half to within ½ inch of the other side. Open like a book. Place between 2 sheets of parchment paper, and pound to an even thickness of about ½ inch with a kitchen mallet.

4 Square up the ends, making roughly a 6-by-9-inch rectangle. On the same work surface,

Sauce

2 Tbsp. bacon fat
½ cup minced leek
2 Tbsp. all-purpose flour
1 cup chicken stock
¼ tsp. poultry seasoning
salt and pepper to taste

1 Pour off all but 2 Tbsp. of the fat from the roasting pan. Place the pan over medium heat on the stovetop, and add the leek. Sauté until softened.

2 Whisk in the flour, and cook for 1 minute. Whisk in the stock and seasonings, and cook for 3 to 4 minutes until thickened. Serve with slices of the bacon-wrapped turkey roast.

weave the bacon with 4 strips vertically placed and weaving in 4 horizontal strips, much as you would with a lattice piecrust, leaving the long ends to wrap.

5 Lay one of the turkey tenderloins in the center of the bacon lattice, spread the leeks over the top to within ½ inch of the edges, and place the second pounded tenderloin on top of that.

6 Shape into a rectangular loaf with your hands, enclosing the leek stuffing. Pull the ends of the bacon over the meat to enclose it.

7 Flip the whole thing onto a shallow roasting pan. Roast for approximately 70 minutes or until the internal temperature reaches 150 degrees F on an instant-read thermometer.

8 Turn the oven to broil, and cook until the bacon is crisped and the internal temperature reaches 165 degrees F — about 5 to 8 minutes.

9 Let rest on a cutting board while making the sauce (above).

Patricia Lehnhardt revels in all things bacon and, while working on recipes and photos for this magazine, visited different grocery stores to avoid depleting their inventories all at once. She shares more recipes at www.thetraveling table.com

Soups & Stews

RECIPES BY
SEPTEMBER MORN

PHOTOS BY
PATRICIA LEHNHARDT

Though most often cast in the role of breakfast meat, a few strips of bacon can really wake up the taste of a soup or stew. A good one deserves to be made in a quantity that allows for leftovers, because the flavors always improve overnight.

These recipes will each make six or more generous servings. If that's more than you and your family can eat at one meal, be glad; the leftovers will taste even better. Also, all three of these dishes will freeze well for quick, delicious, future meals.

The number of slices you use might vary because of your bacon's thickness and quality and its shrinkage while being cooked.

Beef, Beer and Bacon Stew

If you're feeding a houseful of hunters, this stew works great using venison or other game meat in place of beef. It requires a 6-quart slow cooker or a Dutch oven for simmering.

Makes 6 to 8 servings

6 strips bacon
1 Tbsp. bacon drippings
3 lbs. boneless beef, cut into 2-inch chunks
5 cloves garlic, sliced
1 4-inch sprig of rosemary (or 1 tsp. dried)
2 bay leaves
1 tsp. dried basil
½ tsp. black peppercorns
12 oz. beer, any style
1 large onion, sliced
6 medium to large potatoes, cut into 1-inch cubes
6 medium to large carrots, sliced into 3- to 4-inch pieces
3 celery stalks, cut into 1-inch slices
juice and pulp of 1 medium orange
4 to 6 cups water (to cover the ingredients in the pot)

1 Fry the bacon strips until cooked but not crisp; then place them in the bottom of the slow cooker with bacon drippings.

2 Put the beef into the cooker; then add the garlic, rosemary, bay leaves, basil and peppercorns. Add the beer, then the veggies.

3 Add the juice and pulp of the orange. Then add enough water just to cover the ingredients.

4 Put the lid on the slow cooker, and heat on high until the stew reaches a rolling boil. Then turn the temperature to low, and simmer until the meat is tender — about 9 hours.

Note: If you prefer thicker gravy, thicken the stew liquid with cornstarch 1 hour before it's finished cooking. Dissolve 1 Tbsp. cornstarch in ¼ cup cool water; pour this liquid into the simmering stew, and stir.

Cream of Bacon Soup

This soup makes rich comfort food, yet it's loaded with healthy vegetables.

Makes 6 to 8 servings

3 strips bacon
2 Tbsp. bacon drippings
4 celery stalks, sliced
1 small to medium onion, sliced
½ small green pepper, sliced into small pieces
4 cloves garlic, minced
½ cup frozen peas
1 to 2 Tbsp. flour, depending on how thick you want the soup to be
4 cups chicken stock/broth
¼ tsp. black pepper
¼ tsp. cayenne pepper
1 cup heavy cream

1 Fry the bacon until cooked through but not quite crisp. Remove bacon, drain, and set aside.

2 Measure the bacon drippings into a saucepan. Sauté celery, onion, green pepper and garlic for 2 to 3 minutes.

3 Mix the flour into the veggies. Cook 2 minutes, stirring to prevent scorching, until it thickens.

4 Add the chicken broth or stock, a little at a time, mixing it in with a wire whisk to keep lumps from forming. Add black pepper and cayenne. Simmer 10 to 15 minutes to let it thicken, stirring frequently to prevent scorching.

5 Crumble the drained, cooked bacon; then add it and the frozen peas to the simmering pot. Cook for 3 minutes to heat the peas through. Remove the pot from the heat. Mix in the cream, and serve.

Note: If you can't eat the whole batch at once, do NOT add the cream to the pot of soup. Instead, ladle servings into bowls, and add a little cream to each bowl.

Bacon & Black Bean Soup

Black beans are high in protein, fiber and important minerals and low in calories and sodium — plus they support digestive tract health. Even better news: Black beans go great with bacon! Here's a tasty soup that happily combines the two.

Makes 6 to 8 servings

4 strips bacon
1 Tbsp. bacon drippings
1 medium onion, diced
3 cloves garlic, chopped
1 tsp. dry crushed hot pepper
2 15-oz. cans black beans or 3 cups home-cooked
   black beans
1 medium potato, grated
4 cups beef broth, divided
2 tsp. dried basil or 1 Tbsp. fresh chopped
½ lemon, juiced
½ cup red wine
sour cream to garnish

1. Cook the bacon until crispy in the same pot you'll use for the soup, so the cooking flavor will become part of the broth. Drain the bacon, crumble it, and set it aside.

2. Leave 1 Tbsp. bacon drippings in the pot. Sauté the diced onion until it becomes translucent.

3. Add the garlic and hot pepper. Add the black beans, potato and 1 cup beef broth. Bring to a simmer.

4. While it heats, use an electric hand mixer to mash the beans. If you like more texture to your soup, leave some beans whole. If you prefer a purée-style soup, whir the beans in a food processor until smooth before adding them to the pot.

5. Stir in the rest of the beef broth, basil, lemon juice and red wine, and bring to a boil. Simmer about 20 minutes, then serve hot. Garnish with a dollop of sour cream, sprinkled with crumbled bacon.

September Morn lives on a 5-acre hobby farm in western Washington with several Rottweilers that share her enthusiasm about bacon.

Fast

RECIPES AND PHOTOS BY
AMY GRISAK

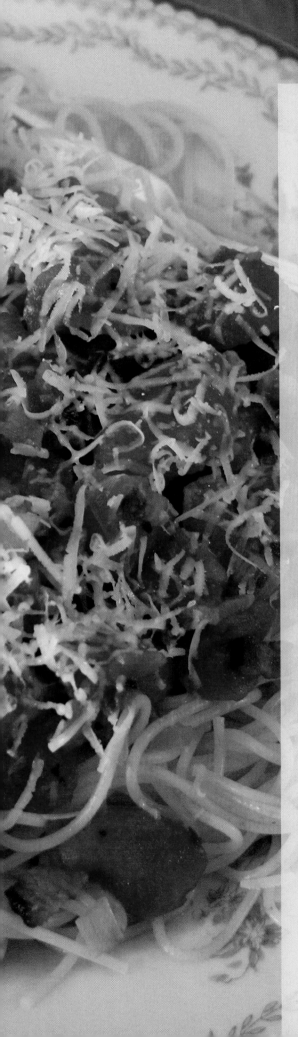

When you have no time in the evening, reach for bacon to create a satisfying meal in a short order. These meals take less than an hour to prepare yet are delicious enough to serve on any special occasion.

Bacon and Tomato Pasta

This is a very warming meal perfect for a midweek supper. Bacon adds heartiness without weighing down the dish, and the red pepper flakes bring out the flavors. With a salad and rustic bread, you have everything you need.

Serves 4

8 bacon slices
2 Tbsp. apple cider vinegar
½ large onion, chopped
½ sweet pepper, chopped
1 28-oz. can diced tomatoes
2 Tbsp. sugar
½ tsp. dried oregano
½ tsp. dried basil
½ tsp. dried thyme
¼ to ½ tsp. red pepper flakes
salt to taste
16 oz. spaghetti or angel hair pasta
freshly grated Parmesan cheese

1. Chop the bacon into ¼-inch pieces. In a large skillet, fry until crisp. Remove from the heat, and place on a paper towel on a plate. Pour off all but 2 Tbsp. of the bacon fat.

2. Add the vinegar to the skillet, and scrap off the brown bits from the bottom of the pan. Add the onion and sweet pepper. Cook on low heat for 2 minutes.

3. Add tomatoes, sugar, herbs, red pepper flakes and bacon. Cook for 10 minutes. Taste, and add salt, if necessary.

4. While the tomatoes cook, boil water for the pasta, and cook the pasta to al dente.

5. Drain the pasta before putting it in a serving dish, spoon over the tomato/bacon mixture, and serve with Parmesan cheese.

Chicken Breasts with Bacon and Mushrooms

Chicken topped with mushrooms and bacon tastes as good as it looks. If you'd like the chicken to cook even faster, you can slice the breasts in half. The chicken pairs well with mashed potatoes, rice or pasta. Add a salad or vegetable side dish, and you have a healthy, fast meal.

Serves 4

8 pieces bacon
salt and pepper
4 chicken breasts
¾ cup chicken broth or dry white wine
4 cups sliced mushrooms
1 tsp. dried thyme

1 Preheat the oven to 350 degrees Fahrenheit. Chop the bacon into ¼-inch pieces. In a large skillet, fry the bacon until it appears crispy. Remove from the heat, and place it on a plate lined with a paper towel.

2 Salt and pepper each side of the chicken breasts, and place them in the pan with the bacon fat. On medium heat, brown them 8 to 10 minutes on each side. Transfer the chicken to a 9-inch-by-13-inch pan.

3 Pour off the bacon grease, leaving 1 Tbsp. Add the chicken broth or white wine. Turn the flame to medium-high, and scrape up the brown bits on the bottom of the pan.

4 Add mushrooms, and cook for 2 minutes. Add thyme and bacon bits. Cook for 1 minute.

5 Pour mushrooms and bacon over chicken. Cover with aluminum foil, and bake for 20 minutes or until the internal temperature of the chicken reaches 165 degrees F.

6 When you serve the chicken, spoon the bacon and mushrooms over the top of the breast.

Bacon and Veggie Frittata

Italians rarely eat eggs for breakfast, but frittatas are a staple at practically any other meal. This is perfect when you have friends who arrive at the last minute, because you can use almost anything in your refrigerator.

Packed with healthy and colorful vegetables along with satisfying eggs and bacon, the recipe is ridiculously easy. Feel free to expand on the variety or the amount of vegetables. The beauty of this dish is you can really use what you have on hand.

Serves 4

8 bacon strips
¼ cup onion, chopped
½ sweet pepper, chopped
1 clove garlic, minced
1 lb. fresh spinach, washed, patted dry and chopped
  into ½-inch strips
8 eggs
½ cup milk
salt and pepper to taste
½ cup grated Parmesan cheese (or any cheese that
  melts well)

1 Preheat the oven to 400 degrees Fahrenheit. Chop the bacon into ¼-inch pieces.

2 In a nonstick, oven-proof skillet, fry the bacon until crisp. Remove the bacon from the heat, and drain on a paper towel-covered plate.

3 Pour off the bacon fat, reserving 2 Tbsp. in the pan. Add the onion, sweet pepper and garlic. Cook on low heat for 2 minutes. Add the spinach, and cook until completely wilted.

4 In a large bowl, whisk together the eggs and milk until frothy. Season with salt and pepper. Pour over the vegetables in the pan, making sure the eggs are evenly distributed over everything.

5 Cook on medium heat for 3 to 5 minutes until the eggs begin to set. Sprinkle the bacon pieces and cheese on the top.

6 Place the skillet in the oven, and cook for 10 minutes, until the eggs are set. After removing it from the oven, rest the frittata for 5 minutes before serving.

Amy Grisak (thebackyardbounty.com) appreciates the pastured hogs raised by friends near her home in Great Falls, Montana, and always looks for ways to work bacon into recipes for her family.

Side Dishes

RECIPES AND PHOTOS
BY NICHOLAS YOUNGINER
AND KEVIN FOGLE

Explore unexpected flavor combinations and try new cuts of bacon with these four creative side dishes that challenge common bacon preconceptions. From a sweet and savory cornbread that features American bacon paired with caramelized onions to the fusion of Asian flavors and jowl bacon in a unique soybean succotash, these innovative side dishes will enliven any meal.

Buttermilk Cornbread with Caramelized Onions and Bacon

This unusual Southern-style savory cornbread is crisped in sizzling bacon fat and laced with smoky bacon and sweet caramelized Vidalia onions.

Serves 6 to 8

½ Tbsp. + ½ cup butter
2 Vidalia onions, diced (or other sweet yellow onion)
3 slices American bacon
⅔ cup white sugar
2 large eggs
1 cup buttermilk
1 cup all-purpose flour
½ tsp. salt
1 cup yellow cornmeal
½ tsp. baking soda

1. Heat a sauté pan on medium-low. Put ½ Tbsp. butter into the pan to melt. Add diced onions, and cover.

2. Cook for 30 minutes, stirring occasionally. The onions are done when they turn a deep-brown color and become sticky and very sweet. Remove from the pan, and set aside.

3. Preheat the oven to 375 degrees Fahrenheit. Heat a 9-inch cast-iron skillet on medium heat.

4. Dice the bacon into ¼-inch squares, and cook in the skillet until crispy and fat is rendered. Set aside the crispy bacon, remove the pan from heat, and leave the rendered fat in the hot skillet.

5. In a microwave or small saucepan, melt the ½ cup of butter. In a mixing bowl, combine the sugar and melted butter. Add eggs, and beat until blended. Add the buttermilk to the egg mixture.

6. In a large mixing bowl, add the flour, salt, cornmeal and baking soda. Whisk to incorporate.

7. Add the buttermilk mixture to the large mixing bowl, stirring just long enough to combine (a few small lumps are OK; overmixing will make the cornbread tough).

8. Once batter has formed, stir in crispy bacon and caramelized onions. Return the skillet with bacon fat to medium heat. Gently pour the batter into the hot skillet, and place into the preheated oven.

9. Bake for 30 to 40 minutes or until a toothpick inserted into the center comes out clean. Cool slightly until warm, and then invert the skillet onto a serving dish to reveal the bacon-crisped edges of the cornbread.

The number of slices you use might vary because of your bacon's thickness and quality and its shrinkage while being cooked.

Asian Succotash

Corn, soybean and guanciale (pig-jowl bacon) highlight this reimagined Southern classic that features scallions, toasted sesame seeds and a light hoisin-based glaze.

Serves 6 to 8

Hoisin glaze
2 Tbsp. rice wine vinegar
3 Tbsp. soy sauce
2 Tbsp. hoisin sauce

Succotash
2 garlic cloves
4 ears sweet corn (yellow or white)
5 slices guanciale
10 oz. bag soybeans, frozen and shelled

Garnish
1 Tbsp. sesame seeds
1 bunch scallions

HOISIN GLAZE

In a small jar with a lid (like a Mason jar), combine the rice wine vinegar, soy sauce and hoisin sauce. Put on the lid, and shake to incorporate the ingredients. Set aside.

SUCCOTASH

Peel and mince the garlic cloves, and set aside. Shuck the corn, and remove the kernels with a knife; to easily cut the kernels, hold the corn vertically on a large cutting board and gently slice the kernels off of the cob. Finally, cut the green tops of the scallions on the bias to create thin angled rounds; set these aside.

GUANCIALE

Heat a sauté pan to medium heat. While the pan is warming up, cut the slices of guanciale into ½-inch-long strips. When the pan is hot, add the guanciale strips, and cook until crispy and the fat has rendered. Remove the strips from the pan, and set aside, leaving fat in the pan.

SUCCOTASH ASSEMBLY

1 Increase the heat of the pan containing the rendered fat to medium-high. Once the pan is hot, add the corn, and sauté until slightly browned.

2 Place the garlic in the pan, and cook until fragrant — about 30 seconds. Add the soybeans, and cook for 3 to 5 minutes until softened. Lightly season the mixture with salt.

3 Pour the hoisin glaze into the pan with the succotash, and toss. Cook for 3 to 5 minutes until the glaze thickens and thoroughly coats the succotash.

4 Finally, add the guanciale slices, toss once more, and remove from the heat.

5 Transfer the succotash to a serving dish, and garnish with sliced scallions and sesame seeds. Serve while warm.

Bacon-y Braised Brussels Sprouts

A classic pairing, these pan-braised Brussels sprouts will turn heads with sweet and smoky notes.

Serves 4

1 lb. Brussels sprouts
3 slices American-bacon
¼ cup pork or chicken stock
1½ Tbsp. Dijon mustard
2 tsp. honey
½ tsp. black pepper

1 Cut the Brussels sprouts in half lengthwise so that the leaves of each half stay together, and set aside.

2 Cut the bacon into 1-inch strips, and place into a sauté pan over medium-high heat. Once the bacon is crisp and fat is rendered, remove the bacon, and reserve the fat in the pan.

3 Place sprouts cut-side down into the pan, and season them lightly with salt. Sear the sprouts for 3 to 5 minutes until brown and crispy on the cut side.

4 Add the stock of your choice to the pan, reduce the heat to medium, and cover. Cook 4 to 5 minutes until the sprouts are tender. Finally, add the mustard, honey and pepper to the pan, and toss to coat the sprouts.

5 Transfer the sprouts to serving dish, and top with the reserved crispy bacon strips. Serve while warm.

Bacon Fat-seared Cabbage with Caraway and Lemon

This dish marries flavors from Germany, America and Ireland to create an amalgamation of flavors — simultaneously succulent and refreshing.

Serves 4

2 heads white cabbage
4 slices American-style bacon
2 tsp. caraway seeds
3 rashers Irish-style bacon or Canadian bacon
2 whole lemons, juiced

1 Roughly chop cabbage into 1- to 1½-inch squares. While chopping, warm a large sauté pan over medium heat.

2 Add the American-style bacon, and cook until crisp and fat has rendered out. Remove the cooked bacon, and either consume it or reserve it for another recipe.

3 Add the caraway seeds and chopped cabbage to the pan with bacon fat, and season with salt.

4 Place a weight (try a flat-bottomed pan that fits inside the sauté pan) directly onto the cabbage to compress it as it cooks. After 5 to 6 minutes, remove the weight, and turn the cabbage so that the nonbrowned pieces can sear. Repeat this process until all of the cabbage is browned and softened.

5 Once the cabbage is completely seared, squeeze the lemon juice onto the cabbage, and stir to incorporate. Cook for 2 minutes, and transfer from the pan into a serving dish. Garnish with the Irish-style bacon.

Nicholas Younginer is a trained chef and nutritional anthropologist based in South Carolina. Kevin Fogle is a freelance writer, photographer and bacon advocate also located in South Carolina.

Irish-style Bacon

1 While the cabbage is cooking, bring another sauté pan to medium-high heat. Cut the Irish-style bacon into strips about 1 inch long, and place in the heated pan.

2 Sear until browned and crisped. Reserve the bacon, and place it on top of the seared cabbage just before serving.

Salads

RECIPES AND PHOTOS BY
FIONA GREEN

While many of us equate bacon with spinach salad, we might not think to add its salty note and crispy texture to other greens. Here are three more options to tease your palate!

Spinach Salad with Bacon, Strawberries, Feta and Honeyed Pecans

This delightful salad pairs fresh, juicy strawberries with crispy bacon, red onion and feta cheese. The addition of sweet, chewy, honeyed pecans provides an extra burst of flavor. While 2 cups of pecans might be more than you need for this recipe, the extras are sure to disappear quickly. This salad is particularly delicious with a light balsamic and olive oil dressing.

Serves 4

Salad
2 cups pecans
¼ cup honey
4 cups baby spinach
6 slices bacon
½ red onion, finely sliced
12 strawberries, halved
1 cup crumbled feta cheese

Dressing
½ cup olive oil
½ cup balsamic vinegar
2 spring onions, finely chopped

1 Preheat the oven to 350 degrees Fahrenheit. Place the pecans on a baking tray, and bake for about 5 minutes or until nicely toasted, taking care to avoid burning. Remove from the oven.

2 Put the honey in a small saucepan, and slowly bring to a boil. Drop the roasted nuts in honey, and stir to coat. Reduce heat, and allow to simmer for 5 minutes; then remove the pan from the stove, and spoon the pecans onto parchment paper, separating them to avoid sticking together.

3 Wash and dry the spinach. Place in a bowl, and set aside.

4 Cook the bacon until crisp, remove from heat, and chop into small pieces. Sprinkle over the spinach.

5 Add the chopped onion, halved strawberries, crumbled feta cheese and honeyed pecans to the bowl.

6 For the dressing: Whisk together the oil and vinegar. Add the onions. Feel free to adjust oil/vinegar ratio according to taste.

Mixed Green Salad with Bacon, Walnuts, Pears and Blue Cheese

The combination of sweet pears, crispy bacon and crunchy walnuts is enhanced by the addition of large chunks of creamy, sharp blue cheese. This hearty salad is one of my favorites. Experiment with different types of pears to find the ones you like best. The delicious dressing blends smooth maple syrup with creamy mustard and chia seeds for a little extra crunch.

Serves 4

6 slices bacon
4 cups mixed greens
2 pears, sliced into thin wedges
½ cup crumbled blue cheese
½ cup walnut pieces
salt and pepper to taste

Maple Mustard Dressing
½ cup mustard
4 Tbsp. maple syrup
1 tsp. lemon juice
¼ cup olive oil
1 Tbsp. chia seeds (optional)
salt and pepper to taste

1 Cook the bacon in a frying pan. When crispy, remove from the heat, and crumble into small pieces.

2 In a large bowl, combine the mixed greens, pear wedges and crumbled blue cheese. Add the bacon and walnut pieces.

3 To make the dressing: Pour all ingredients into a jar, close the lid, and shake until blended.

Bacon and Grilled Peach Salad

Nothing says summer like a grilled peach salad. In this recipe, romaine lettuce is topped with mozzarella balls, delicious Canadian bacon and fresh peaches grilled to perfection. A light citrus-mint dressing enhances the flavor, while crispy sliced almonds offer more protein.

Serves 4

8 slices Canadian bacon
4 peaches
olive oil to spritz
4 cups finely chopped romaine lettuce
½ cup mozzarella balls
¼ cup sliced almonds
salt and pepper to taste

Citrus Mint Dressing
¾ cup orange juice
1 tsp. lemon juice
3 Tbsp. olive oil
1 Tbsp. apple cider vinegar
2 Tbsp. mustard
2 tsp. fresh mint, chopped

Optional: ¼ cup balsamic reduction

1 Fry or grill the bacon, and cut into small pieces.

2 Quarter the peaches, and lightly spritz with olive oil. Arrange on a baking tray, and grill or broil in the oven for 5 minutes. Remove from heat.

3 Divide the romaine lettuce between 4 bowls. Divide the bacon, peaches and mozzarella balls evenly between the bowls. Sprinkle the almonds on top.

4 For the dressing: Place all of the ingredients in a jar, close the lid, and shake well until combined.

5 If desired, drizzle balsamic reduction over the final product for a salad that tastes as great as it looks.

Bacon and Shrimp Kale Salad

If you can't decide between shrimp or bacon, enjoy both in this tasty salad, which features lime-marinated shrimp and grilled bacon. A tangy lime-ginger dressing makes an excellent partner for this salad.

Serves 4

2 Tbsp. olive oil
8 Tbsp. lime juice
1 garlic clove, minced (optional)
16 raw shrimp
8 slices bacon
4 cups kale
20 halved cherry tomatoes
2 avocados, chopped
pinch of black pepper
pinch of salt

Dressing
½ cup olive oil
½ cup lime juice
1 tsp. mustard
1 Tbsp. minced ginger
1 Tbsp. sesame seeds
2 Tbsp. water
½ tsp. black pepper

1 Preheat the oven to 350 degrees Fahrenheit.

2 Create the marinade by mixing together the olive oil, lime juice and garlic (if desired). Wash the shrimp; then place in the marinade for 20 minutes.

3 Place a sheet of aluminum foil on a cookie sheet. Remove the shrimp from the marinade, and lay on the cookie sheet. Cook on the oven's middle shelf for 12 minutes, turning halfway through the cooking time. Remove from the oven.

4 Meanwhile, fry the bacon until crispy, remove from the heat, and cut into pieces.

5 Wash and chop kale; drain it, and place in a bowl. Add tomatoes and avocado. Top with bacon and shrimp.

6 For the dressing: Place all of the ingredients in a small bowl, and whisk with a fork until well blended.

When she's not rescuing homeless animals or running half marathons, Fiona Green can be found in her kitchen, concocting delicious dishes like the ones in this magazine.

How many pieces of bacon are consumed in America each year?
A. 100 million
B. 50 million
C. 250,000
D. 32 billion
Answer: D. 32 BILLION pieces of bacon are eaten each year.

Desserts

RECIPES BY **ASHLEY ENGLISH**
PHOTOS BY
PATRICIA LEHNHARDT

It's long been said that everything goes better with bacon (at least around my house, that is!). Why not extend that mindset to dessert? With its meaty, salty, sweet trifecta, bacon is a perfect ingredient for rendering into a treat. Here I've tucked it into a galette, a blondie, a bark and a bread pudding. After sampling these desserts, don't be surprised if you find yourself looking for ways to add bacon to every sweet dish you make!

Spiced Apple & Candied Maple Bacon Galette

Here bacon is first dredged in maple syrup, then baked until crispy. The resulting sweet and salty flavor is a perfect complement to the tart bite of Granny Smith apples.

Serves 6 to 8

Crust
1¼ cups all-purpose flour
¾ tsp. salt
½ cup butter (1 stick), chilled and cubed
⅓ cup ice water

Bacon
4 slices thick-cut or 6 slices regular bacon
¼ cup maple syrup

Filling
½ cup sugar
¼ cup arrowroot powder or cornstarch
5 Granny Smith apples, peeled, cored and cut into thin slices
½ tsp. cinnamon
½ tsp. ground ginger
¼ tsp. ground allspice
¼ tsp. salt

1 Mix the flour and salt in a medium-large mixing bowl. Using a pastry cutter or two forks, incorporate the butter until the mixture resembles a coarse meal. (You should have rather large bits of butter when you have finished.)

2 Slowly drizzle in the ice water. Stir with a mixing spoon until the dough starts to clump.

3 Transfer the dough onto a floured work surface, and fold it into itself with your hands. The galette dough should come together easily but should not feel overly sticky.

4 Form the dough into a flattened disk. Wrap it in cellophane, and refrigerate for at least 1 hour.

5 Remove the chilled dough from the refrigerator. Using a rolling pin, flatten it into a 12-inch circle on a lightly floured surface.

6 Transfer the pastry dough to a large baking dish, lined with a silicone baking mat or lightly buttered. Place the baking dish in the refrigerator while preparing the filling.

7 Preheat the oven to 375 degrees Fahrenheit. Place a cooling rack above a rimmed baking pan.

8 Place the maple syrup in a shallow bowl. Pick up a slice of bacon, and gently rub it into the syrup. Flip it, and repeat on the other side.

9 Transfer the bacon strip to the cooling rack; repeat with the remaining slices. Bake for 15 to 20 minutes for regular slices or 25 to 30 minutes for thick-cut slices — until the bacon looks crispy and darkened.

10 Remove the baking pan from the oven. Cool until easy to handle. Cut the bacon into matchstick-size pieces. Set aside.

11 Combine sugar and arrowroot powder or cornstarch in a medium-sized mixing bowl. Add the apple slices, spices and salt. Using either clean hands or a mixing spoon, toss all ingredients together.

12 Remove the baking dish from the refrigerator, and fan out the apple mixture atop the chilled dough, leaving a 2-inch border. Fold the border to overlap the filling, and press folds together every few inches.

13 Bake for 55 for 60 minutes, until the crust is golden and the filling bubbles in the center. Remove from the oven, and cool slightly.

14 Scatter the cut pieces of bacon across the surface of the galette. Cool at least 30 minutes before serving.

Bacon Blondies

As much as I love blondies, I sometimes find them a bit one-note. All that sweetness needs a bit of tempering, and it turns out that the smoky hint provided by bacon is the perfect solution.

Serves 9 to 12

3 slices thick-cut or 5 slices regular bacon
8 Tbsp. butter, melted
¾ cup light brown sugar
¼ cup sugar
1 large egg
2 tsp. vanilla extract
1 cup all-purpose flour
½ tsp. salt
¾ cup chocolate chips

1 Butter an 8-by-8-inch baking dish. Set aside.

2 Preheat the oven to 375 degrees Fahrenheit. Place a cooling rack above a rimmed baking pan.

3 Lay the bacon slices atop the cooling rack. Bake for 15 to 20 minutes for regular slices or 25 to 30 minutes for thick-cut slices — until the bacon looks crispy and darkened.

4 Remove from oven, and cool until easy to handle. Chop the cooked bacon into small pieces. Set aside. Reduce the oven temperature to 350 degrees F.

5 Using an electric mixer, beat the melted butter and sugars together until smooth and fluffy, about 3 to 4 minutes. Add the egg and vanilla; beat until well incorporated.

6 Add the flour and salt, beating until well blended. Stir in the chocolate chips and bacon pieces.

7 Transfer the mixture to the buttered dish. Spread evenly with a spatula.

8 Bake for about 25 to 30 minutes, until the top is golden and a knife inserted into the center of the pan comes out clean. Cool for 15 minutes prior to serving.

The number of slices you use might vary because of your bacon's thickness and quality and its shrinkage while being cooked.

Bacon, Cranberry & Pecan Chocolate Bark

This bark will quickly become your go-to holiday gift-giving confection. It comes together quite quickly and offers sweet, salty, tart and crunchy flavors and textures to please every palate.

Makes 1½ lbs.

4 slices thick-cut or 6 slices regular bacon
1 lb. dark chocolate (60 percent cacao or higher)
1 cup toasted and chopped pecans
½ cup dried cranberries

1 Line a 10-by-15-inch rimmed baking pan (also called a "jelly roll pan") with wax paper. Set aside.

2 Preheat the oven to 375 degrees Fahrenheit. Place a cooling rack above a rimmed baking pan.

3 Lay the bacon slices atop the cooling rack. Bake for 15 to 20 minutes for regular slices or 25 to 30 minutes for thick-cut slices — until the bacon looks crispy and darkened.

4 Remove the baking pan from the oven. Cool until easy to handle. Coarsely chop the slices into small pieces. Set aside.

5 Melt the chocolate in a double boiler, stirring constantly. If you don't have a double boiler, you can set a metal or glass mixing bowl atop a pot filled with 2 inches of water, taking care that the water doesn't touch the bottom of the bowl.

6 After the chocolate melts, stir in half of the pecans, cranberries and bacon. Pour the mixture atop the wax paper, using a spatula to spread it out. Sprinkle half of the pecans, cranberries and bacon over the surface of the chocolate, pressing gently with your hands so they adhere to the surface.

7 Place the pan in the refrigerator for 3 to 4 hours to cool. Cut the bark into your preferred sizes. Store in a lidded container in the refrigerator, and consume within 2 to 3 days.

Dried Cherry & Bacon Bread Pudding

While intended for dessert, this bread pudding is substantive enough for breakfast. If you opt to add whipped cream, I highly suggest spiking it with a bit of bourbon or whiskey for an added layer of flavor.

Serves 8 to 10

6 slices thick-cut or 8 slices regular bacon
1 loaf challah bread (1 to 1½ pounds), cut into 1-inch cubes
1 cup dried cherries
6 eggs
4 cups milk
1½ cups heavy cream
¾ cup sugar
1 Tbsp. vanilla extract
1 tsp. cinnamon
pinch of salt

1 Butter a 9-by-13-inch high-sided baking dish. Set aside.

2 Preheat the oven to 375 degrees Fahrenheit. Place a cooling rack above a rimmed baking pan.

3 Lay the bacon slices atop the cooling rack. Bake for 15 to 20 minutes for regular slices or 25-30 minutes for thick-cut slices — until the bacon looks crispy and darkened.

4 Remove the baking pan from the oven. Cool until easy to handle. Using your hands, tear the strips into rough, medium-size pieces. Set aside. Reduce the oven temperature to 350 degrees F.

5 Place the cubed challah in the prepared baking dish. Pour the dried cherries and bacon pieces over the bread. Using your hands, toss to distribute the ingredients throughout the bread cubes.

6 In a medium-size mixing bowl, beat the eggs until fluffy. Add the milk, cream, sugar, vanilla, cinnamon and salt. Beat until fully incorporated.

7 Pour the custard over the bread mixture. Use a metal spoon or spatula to coat the cubes. Set the pan aside to soak for 30 minutes.

8 Bake for 1 hour, until the top is golden and the custard mixture has become firm. Remove from the oven, and cool at least 15 minutes before serving. While delicious on its own, it also tastes great with whipped cream or ice cream.

Chocoholics and bacon lovers both rejoice over the creation of a county fair favorite, chocolate-covered bacon, as well as the gourmet chocolate bars created by Vosges. For $7.50, you can have a decadent treat with hickory-smoked bacon and Alderwood-smoked salt in 41 percent milk chocolate or 62 percent dark chocolate.

Beverages

RECIPES AND PHOTOS BY
PATRICIA LEHNHARDT

You definitely want to include these drinks in your repertoire. Bacon-infused alcohol transforms all your cocktails, and bacon-infused hot chocolate or milkshakes will delight your family. Here are plenty of bacon accoutrements to dress up the glass and enhance the salty, smoky flavors we crave.

Bacon, Bacon, Bacon Bloody Mary

Bacon on the rim of the glass, bacon in the vodka, bacon in the olive garnish ... Let the party begin!

Serves 4

For each drink:
2 oz. bacon-infused vodka
½ cup Bloody Mary mix
1 bacon-rimmed glass
ice cubes to fill the glass ¾ full
2 fried bacon-stuffed olives on a skewer
1 leafy, inner celery stalk

Combine the vodka and the mix, and pour over ice in a bacon-rimmed glass. Garnish with olives and celery.

Bacon-infused Vodka
¼ cup melted bacon fat
1 cup vodka

1. Stir together the warm fat and vodka. Cover and store at room temperature for 48 hours.

2. Refrigerate for several hours, until the fat is solid. Pour through a fine mesh strainer. The fat can be deliciously used to fry burgers.

Bloody Mary Mix
2 cups tomato juice
2 Tbsp. horseradish
4 to 6 dashes hot sauce (such as Tabasco)
1 Tbsp. Worcestershire sauce
1 tsp. celery salt
2 Tbsp. green olive brine from the jar
3 Tbsp. lemon juice

Combine in a pitcher, cover, and chill.

Fried Bacon-stuffed Olives
2 strips bacon, fried until crisp and finely chopped
3 Tbsp. cream cheese

⅛ tsp. chipotle chili powder
8 jumbo green olives, pitted
2 Tbsp. all-purpose flour
1 small egg, beaten
⅓ cup panko breadcrumbs
2 cups peanut oil

1. In a small bowl, combine the bacon, cream cheese and chipotle chili powder. Stuff the bacon-cheese mixture into the olives with a small spoon.

2. Set up the breading station with 3 shallow bowls: 1 with flour, 1 with egg and 1 with breadcrumbs. Roll the olives in flour, then egg and then breadcrumbs, pressing so the crumbs adhere. Refrigerate until ready to fry.

3. In a small pot, heat the oil to 350 degrees Fahrenheit. Fry 6 olives at a time until golden-brown — about a minute per batch. Drain on paper towels.

Bacon-rimmed Glass

1 strip crisp-fried bacon
½ lemon

In a small food processor, grind the strip of crisp bacon until very fine. Rub the rim of 1 of 4 glasses with the lemon, and dip the rim of the glass in the bacon. Set aside to dry.

Hot Chocolate Mix

8 oz. bittersweet chocolate, chopped
½ cup cocoa powder
¼ cup sugar

In a food processor, grind the chocolate until fine. Add the cocoa and sugar, and process until thoroughly mixed. Store in an airtight container.

Bacon Hot Chocolate with Bacon Marshmallows

Chocolate and bacon are the perfect combination, so why not gussy up your favorite cold weather treat? Bacon marshmallows take it over the top — or if you're not in the mood to make them, just add a slice of candied bacon to garnish, and enjoy.

Serves 2

2 cups whole milk
2 strips extra-smoky bacon, fried crisp and well-drained on paper towels, broken into pieces
½ cup hot chocolate mix
¼ cup water
2 to 3 bacon marshmallows

Bacon Marshmallows

Makes 24

½ cup confectioners' sugar
¼ cup cornstarch
2¼ tsp. unflavored powdered gelatin
¼ cup water
⅓ cup sugar
¼ cup maple syrup
2 Tbsp. light corn syrup
2 Tbsp. water
pinch of salt
⅓ cup finely chopped candied bacon (see page 93)

1 Sift the confectioners' sugar and cornstarch together.

2 Spray a 5-inch-by-8-inch loaf pan with nonstick baking spray, or sprinkle a sheet pan heavily with the confectioners' sugar-cornstarch mixture if piping the marshmallows (see step 8).

3 In a medium-sized microwave-proof mixing bowl, stir together the gelatin and water. Let soak for 5 minutes. Microwave on high for 20 to 30 seconds or until completely melted.

4 In a small saucepan, combine the sugar, maple syrup, corn syrup, water and salt. Bring to a boil, and cook until the temperature registers 240 degrees Fahrenheit on a candy thermometer.

5 With an electric mixer, beat the gelatin mixture while slowly adding the sugar mixture. Continue beating on high for 5 minutes, until the marshmallows are thick, creamy and cool.

6 Immediately stir in the bacon, and pour into the prepared pan. Sift the confectioners' sugar and cornstarch over the top in a thick layer, reserving enough to dust a cutting board and roll the marshmallows. Let sit at room temperature for 8 hours.

7 Turn out the marshmallow onto a sugar-cornstarch dusted cutting board. Cut into squares, and roll in additional sugar-cornstarch so all sides are covered and won't stick together. Store in an airtight container for up to 5 days.

8 The marshmallows also can be piped with a decorative tip in a pastry bag onto a sugar-cornstarch dusted sheet pan and allowed to dry overnight. Sift more sugar-cornstarch over the top. Store in an airtight container up to 5 days.

1 In a saucepan, heat the milk and bacon to just below simmering. Turn off the heat, cover, and let steep for 30 minutes to infuse the flavor of the bacon into the milk.

2 In a separate saucepan, combine the hot chocolate mix with water, and bring to a boil, whisking constantly until the chocolate melts smoothly.

3 Strain the milk into the chocolate, whisk, and reheat until steaming. Serve with bacon marshmallows or a candied bacon skewer (see page 93).

Bacon Caramel Milkshake

Chocolate, bacon, peanuts, caramel, cream...what more could you ask for? This is a decadent treat with all your favorite flavors!

Makes 1 large shake — easily multiplied

Garnish
3 Tbsp. heavy cream, divided
2 Tbsp. caramel bits
1 tsp. mini chocolate chips
2 tsp. salted peanuts, chopped

Shake
2 strips candied bacon (see page 93)
2 Tbsp. mini chocolate chips
2 Tbsp. caramel bits or chopped caramels
2 Tbsp. salted peanuts
1 cup chocolate ice cream
½ cup milk

1 Whip 2 Tbsp. cream until stiff. Melt the caramel bits with remaining 1 Tbsp. cream in the microwave (about 30 seconds), and stir until smooth.

2 Cut the end off one of the bacon strips to use as a garnish, and chop the rest. In the bowl of a food processor, mix the chopped bacon, chocolate chips, caramel and peanuts until finely ground.

3 Add the ice cream and milk, and process until smooth. Pour into a glass, and garnish with a dollop of whipped cream, chocolate chips, chopped peanuts, drizzle of caramel and piece of candied bacon.

Orange Bacon Bourbon Cocktail

The rich flavor of bourbon is enhanced by smoky bacon and highlighted with a lift of orange.

Makes 1 drink — easily multiplied

2 oz. bacon-infused bourbon (see below)
½ oz. triple sec
dash of bitters
ice cubes
orange-peel twist
1 strip candied bacon, in roll, or twisted into a rope
(see recipe to the right)

1 In a glass, mix the bourbon, triple sec and bitters. Serve straight up or over ice with an orange twist and bacon garnish.

Patricia Lehnhardt revels in all things bacon and, while working on recipes and photos for this magazine, visited different grocery stores to avoid depleting their inventories all at once. She shares more recipes at www.thetravelingtable.com

Candied Bacon

6 strips thin-cut bacon
¼ cup brown sugar

1 Preheat oven to 350 degrees Fahrenheit. Prepare a baking sheet by lining it with aluminum foil.

2 Spread the brown sugar on a plate. Press each strip of bacon onto the sugar, helping it to adhere. Brush off any excess, and lay bacon on the baking sheet.

3 Bake for 15 minutes. Flip over the bacon, and bake 8 to 10 minutes until crisp and dark golden-brown. Watch carefully toward the end, as it can easily burn. Transfer the bacon to a rack to cool and crisp.

Notes: Add flavor to the brown sugar with a pinch of cinnamon, chipotle powder or citrus zest. When the bacon comes out of the oven and is pliable, you can wrap it around the handle of a wooden spoon or utensil to create a roll or coil, or twist to make a rope.

Bacon Bourbon

¼ cup melted bacon fat
1 cup bourbon

1 Combine bacon fat and bourbon. Cover, and let stand at room temperature for 48 hours.

2 Refrigerate until the fat solidifies, and pour through a fine mesh strainer. Reserve the fat for frying burgers.

amazing grease

waste-not-want-not

living is more popular than ever. Homemakers and cooks are rediscovering the wisdom of generations past and making it our own. Raising chickens or growing an abundant vegetable garden might seem daunting, but saving and reusing byproducts of things we already love to make? Brilliant! Few byproducts are as delicious and useful as bacon grease.

Recipe-enhancing Goodness

Bacon drippings can be substituted for cooking oils, shortening and butter in virtually any recipe. The possibilities are limited only by the imagination — and individual taste. Make bacon-flavored stovetop popcorn for movie night. Coat skillets and cast-iron appliances for savory pancakes, waffles and panini.

One of my favorite instant turnarounds is adding the leftover grease and bits from oven-cooked

bacon to honey cornbread batter and reusing the foil to line the baking pan. The result is an unbelievably yummy crust on the bottom of the cornbread — a perfect combination with spicy chili or hearty bean soup.

If you love sweet and savory flavors together, try adding bacon grease to pastry crusts, cobblers and crumble toppings for baked fruit desserts. Its flavor pairs especially well with apples and peaches.

Check out some surprising uses for bacon drippings!

BY JENNIFER DODD

Try adding bacon drippings to your pastry crusts.

ARINA P HABICH/SHUTTERSTOCK

For a fail-proof, crowd-pleasing macaroni and cheese, don't just add bacon bits; swap some of the butter in the sauce with bacon drippings for even more flavor. Mashed potatoes, sautéed mushrooms, hash browns, homemade salad dressing and more can be transformed into bacony delights.

Nibbles for Fur and Feathers

As commercials have reminded us for years, dogs love bacon. Drizzling their dry food with leftover drippings is a special treat that helps keep coats shiny. A drop or two on bread wrapped over pills can make their medicine go down more happily. (As always, ask your veterinarian before making any dietary changes.)

Wild birds are crazy for bacon flavor, too. Combine grease with cracked corn, shelled peanuts, and sunflower, millet and nyjer to make suet cakes for them — or simply pour grease over pine cones, roll them in bird seed, and hang outside to attract winged visitors to your yard.

Easy Household Helps

Strained through a coffee filter and stored in the refrigerator, bacon grease can be used anytime for many fixes around the house. Out of leather polish? A bit of grease on a cotton cloth can shine and soften shoes, belts, purses and other leather items. (Try a test patch first to avoid unexpected effects on favorite items.)

Pestered by bugs? Mix grease with vegetable oil and sugar, pour into empty cans or onto disposable plates, and set out. Unwanted creepy-crawlies will be attracted by the sweet and savory smell and get trapped in the sticky solution.

Need help with the fireplace or chiminea? Make your own fire starters. Roll up a paper towel, put it in a paper cup, and pour in a little grease. Leave in the refrigerator to allow the paper towel to soak up — and to keep the grease from going rancid over time — then use as you would other firestarters to get a nice blaze going.

TAMARA KULIKOVA/SHUTTERSTOCK

You can enjoy the scent of bacon after melting wax and bacon drippings to make candles.

Want a smaller warm glow? Create simple candles: Purchase wicks and kitchen wax from a craft- or candle-supply company. Place wicks in clean, empty glass jars. Add 1 part wax to 5 parts bacon grease in a large glass bowl. Heat it double-boiler style with hot water, and stir until the melted wax and liquefied grease are well mixed. Carefully pour into the prepared glass jars. When lit, the candles will fill your room with a subtle, mouthwatering bacon aroma. Don't forget to make extras as fun gifts for bacon-loving friends and family.

Homespun Health and Beauty

If you're tired of products with unpronounceable chemicals filling your bathroom cabinets, craft your own from everyday kitchen ingredients. To purify bacon grease for use in bath and body recipes, bring 2 parts water and 1 part grease to a slow boil on the stovetop. Let it simmer until the mixture clarifies and reduces in volume (about 30 to 60 minutes). Leave it in the refrigerator overnight; then separate the solid fat from the liquidy waste at the bottom of the cooled pot.

Use the purified grease with water and lye to make beautifully sudsy soap. Coax out a stubborn splinter by spreading grease over it and covering with an adhesive bandage for a few hours. Apply grease directly to rough or cracked skin for deep moisturizing.

With so many amazing possibilities, Grandma's treasured grease can is making a comeback. Don't toss that bacon grease. Use it!

Jennifer Dodd works in higher education in a small mountain town in Southern California. She loves reading, gardening and — of course — exploring the wonders of bacon.

"Bacon is remarkably versatile. Few foods are as satisfying when munched on their own or have the ability to enhance the flavor of so many other foods the way bacon does." — Jayne Rockmill, "I Love Bacon" (Andrews McMeel Publishing)